Not with a Bang But a Whimper

Not with a Bang But a Whimper

The Politics and Culture of Decline

THEODORE DALRYMPLE

Ivan R. Dee

CHICAGO 2008

www.ivanrdee.com

Most of the contents of this book first appeared in *City Journal*,
published by the Manhattan Institute.

Library of Congress Cataloging-in-Publication Data:
Dalrymple, Theodore.
    Not with a bang but a whimper : the politics and culture of decline /
Theodore Dalrymple.
        p. cm.
    Includes index.
    ISBN-13: 978-1-56663-795-4 (cloth : alk. paper)
    ISBN-10: 1-56663-795-3 (cloth : alk. paper)
    1. Politics and culture. 2. Culture—Philosophy. I. Title.
HM621.D34 2008
    306.201—dc22   2008006500

To the memory of my parents

Contents

Preface

◈ NO AGE is golden to those who live in it, and it is not often in human history that men are more grateful for past
progress than worried by current imperfections.

Even so, our current age seems exceptional in the peculiar-
ity of its unease. Never in human history have people lived such
long and pain-free lives; never have so many people, and so high
a proportion of people, had so much freedom to choose how to
live, what goals to pursue, and how to divert themselves. On the
other hand, never have so many people felt anxious and de-
pressed, and resorted to pills to ease their distress. Mankind has
labored long and hard to produce a cornucopia for itself, only
to discover that the cornucopia does not bring the happiness expected, but only a different kind of anxiety.

Of all modern societies, none is more emblematic of this
strange disconnection between prosperity and its expected benefits than Britain. The country has experienced continuous economic growth for many years and, however illusory or highly
mortgaged that prosperity has been, levels of consumption have
risen enormously. And yet it takes very little familiarity with
Britain to realize that it suffers from a deep malaise, such that
at least half the population would rather live somewhere else.
While people pour in from Eastern Europe, Africa, South Asia,
the Middle East, and (to a lesser extent) South America, in order to earn more money, the population already there seek in

large numbers to move to North America, Australasia, and the Mediterranean.

Increased levels of consumption have not translated into improvement in subjective quality of life. The country is crime-ridden, and the authorities seem impotent, unwilling or unable to do anything about it. Every day come stories of grotesque failure on the part of the criminal justice system. Quotidian encounters between citizens take on an ever more aggressive timbre. Officialdom interferes in daily lives ever more obtrusively while the public administration seems to be a giant machine efficient only in grinding taxes out of people without returning anything in the way of improved services or infrastructure. The sturdy independent upright citizen has become a neurotic dependent frightened wreck. The state is experienced as a juggernaut that cannot be stopped and is no longer under anyone's control. Politicians of all stripes are derided as liars and careerists, ex officio, and cynicism about every official's motives is rife. No official explanation of anything is believed, and honesty, straightforwardness, and trust have become symptoms of naiveté and lack of sophistication. All these traits are mirror images of what, not so very long ago, were the country's virtues.

Perhaps no statistic captures the malaise better than one I saw reported recently in the *Guardian* newspaper, that 79 percent of British children now have a personal television in their bedroom (the 21 percent who don't probably feel resentful and deprived). On the one hand this appears to be a sign of tremendous prosperity, that so high a proportion of the population can now afford to give its children a piece of apparatus that would once have made kings gasp with amazement; but on the other, it raises suspicions that children are spending so much time in front of screens that something human, namely ordinary face-to-face contact, is being undermined or lost. Parents feels constrained, apparently, to give each child a television (and a computer) in order to avoid disputes over who watches what, in the process depriving their children of normal play and imbuing them with a bogus sophistication, that is to say, with knowingness rather than knowledge.

On practically all measures of social pathology, Britain leads the Western world, though only half a century ago it was better ordered as well as freer than most other societies. There is no mistake its governments have made, or errors its intellectuals have propounded, that the government and intellectuals of other countries could not make or propound.

The United States is not immune from the collapse of confidence that underlies the deep British malaise. It is as plentifully supplied as Britain with intellectuals who indulge in cultural self-doubt, more from a desire to present themselves to their peers as broad-minded than from any love of truth or wisdom. And the United States is entering a difficult period, when its relative economic and political power might be in decline. It is one thing to indulge in exhibitionist self-doubt when you are in a position of strength, and another when you are not. What has happened in Britain is a warning; and a warning is a beacon of sorts.

Not with a Bang But a Whimper

ARTISTS AND
IDEOLOGUES

The Gift of Language

◈ NOW THAT I'VE RETIRED early from medical practice in a slum hospital and the prison next door, my former colleagues sometimes ask me, not without a trace of anxiety, whether I think I made the right choice or whether I miss my previous life. They are good friends and fine men, but it is only human nature not to wish unalloyed happiness to one who has chosen a path that diverges, even slightly, from one's own.

Fortunately, I do miss some aspects of my work: if I didn't, it would mean that I had not enjoyed what I did for many years and had wasted a large stretch of my life. I miss, for instance, the sudden illumination into the worldview of my patients that their replies to simple questions sometimes gave me. I still do a certain amount of medico-legal work, preparing psychiatric reports on those accused of crimes, and recently a case reminded me of how sharply a few words can bring into relief an entire attitude toward life and shed light on an entire mental hinterland.

A young woman was charged with assault, under the influence of alcohol and marijuana, on a very old lady about five times her age. Describing her childhood, the young accused mentioned that her mother had once been in trouble with the police.

"What for?" I asked.

"She was on the Social [Security] and working at the same time."

"What happened?" I asked.

"She had to give up working." The air of self-evidence with which she said this revealed a whole world of presuppositions. For her, and those around her, work was the last resort; economic dependence on state handouts was the natural condition of man.

I delighted in what my patients said. One of them always laced his statements with proverbs, which he invariably mangled. "Sometimes, doctor," he said to me one day, "I feel like the little boy with his finger in the dike, crying wolf." And I enjoyed the expressive argot of prison. The prison officers, too, had their own language. They called a loquacious prisoner "verbal" if they believed him to be mad, and "mouthy" if they believed him to be merely bad and willfully misbehaving.

Brief exchanges could so entertain me that on occasion they transformed duty into pleasure. Once I was called to the prison in the early hours to examine a man who had just tried to hang himself. He was sitting in a room with a prison officer. It was about three in the morning, the very worst time to be roused from sleep.

"The things you have to do for Umanity, sir," said the prison officer to me.

The prisoner, looking bemused, said to him, "You what?"

"U-manity," said the prison officer, turning to the prisoner. "You're Uman, aren't you?"

It was like living in a glorious comic passage in Dickens.

For the most part, though, I was struck not by the verbal felicity and invention of my patients and those around them but by their inability to express themselves with anything like facility: and this after eleven years of compulsory education, or (more accurately) attendance at school.

With a very limited vocabulary, it is impossible to make, or at least to express, important distinctions and to examine any question with conceptual care. My patients often had no words to describe what they were feeling, except in the crudest possible way, with expostulations, exclamations, and physical displays of emotion. Often, by guesswork and my experience of other patients, I could put things into words for them, words that they grasped at eagerly. Everything was on the tip of their tongue, rarely or never reaching the stage of expression out loud. They struggled even to describe in a consecutive and logical fashion what had happened to them, at least without a great deal of prompting. Complex narrative and most abstractions were closed to them.

In their dealings with authority, they were at a huge disadvantage—a disaster, since so many of them depended upon various public bureaucracies for so many of their needs, from their housing and health care to their income and the education of their children. I would find myself dealing on their behalf with those bureaucracies, which were often simultaneously bullying and incompetent; and what officialdom had claimed for months or even years to be impossible suddenly, on my intervention, became possible within a week. Of course it was not my mastery of language alone that produced this result; rather, my mastery of language signaled my capacity to make serious trouble for the bureaucrats if they did not do as I asked. I do not think it is a coincidence that the offices of all those bureaucracies were increasingly installing security barriers against the physical attacks on the staff by enraged but inarticulate dependents.

All this, it seems to me, directly contradicts our era's ruling orthodoxy about language. According to that orthodoxy, every child, save the severely brain-damaged and those with very rare genetic defects, learns his or her native language with perfect facility, adequate to his needs. He does so because the faculty of language is part of human nature, inscribed in man's physical being, as it were, and almost independent of environment. To be sure, today's language theorists concede that if a child grows up completely isolated from other human beings until the age of about six, he will never learn language adequately; but this very fact, they argue, implies that the capacity for language is "hard-wired" into the human brain, to be activated only at a certain stage in each individual's development, which in turn proves that language is an inherent biological characteristic of mankind rather than a merely cultural artifact. Moreover language itself is always rule-governed; and the rules that govern it are universally the same, when stripped of certain minor incidentals and contingencies that superficially appear important but in reality are not.

It follows that no language or dialect is superior to any other and that modes of verbal communication cannot be ranked according to complexity, expressiveness, or any other virtue. Thus attempts to foist alleged grammatical "correctness" on native speakers of an "incorrect" dialect are nothing but the unacknowledged and oppressive exercise of social control—the means by which the elites deprive whole social classes and peoples of self-esteem and keep them in permanent subordination. If they are convinced that they can't speak their own language properly, how can they possibly feel other than unworthy, humiliated, and disfranchised? Hence the refusal to teach formal grammar is both in accord with a correct understanding of the nature of language and is politically generous, inasmuch as it confers equal status on all forms of speech and therefore upon all speakers.

The *locus classicus* of this way of thinking, at least for laymen such as myself, is Steven Pinker's book *The Language Instinct*. A best-seller when first published in 1994, it is now in its twenty-fifth printing in the British paperback version alone, and its wide circulation suggests a broad influence on the opinions of the intelligent public. Pinker is a professor of psychology at Harvard University, and that institution's great prestige cloaks him, too, in the eyes of many. If Professor Pinker were not right on so important a subject, which is one to which he has devoted much study and brilliant intelligence, would he have tenure at Harvard?

Pinker nails his colors to the mast at once. His book, he says, "will not chide you about proper usage" because, after all, "[l]anguage is a complex, specialized skill, which . . . is qualitatively the same in every individual. . . . Language is no more a cultural invention than is upright posture," and men are as naturally equal in their ability to express themselves as in their ability to stand on two legs. "Once you begin to look at language . . . as a biological adaptation to communicate information," Pinker continues, "it is no longer as tempting to see language as an insidious shaper of thought." Every individual has an equal linguistic capacity to formulate the most complex and refined thoughts. We all have, so to speak, the same tools for thinking. "When it comes to linguistic form," Pinker says, quoting the anthropologist Edward Sapir, "Plato walks with the Macedonian swineherd, Confucius with the head-hunting savage of Assam." To put it another way, "linguistic genius is involved every time a child learns his or her mother tongue."

The old-fashioned and elitist idea that there is a "correct" and "incorrect" form of language no doubt explains the fact that "[l]inguists repeatedly run up against the myth that working-class people . . . speak a simpler and a coarser language. This is a pernicious illusion. . . . Trifling differences between the dialect of the mainstream and the dialect of other groups . . . are dignified as badges of 'proper grammar.'" These are, in fact, the "hobgoblins of the schoolmarm," and ipso facto contemptible. In fact standard English is one of those languages that "is a dialect with an army and a navy." The schoolmarms he so slightingly dismisses are in fact but the linguistic arm of a colonial power—the middle class—oppressing what would otherwise be a much freer and happier populace. "Since prescriptive rules are so psychologically unnatural that only those with access to the right schooling can abide by them, they serve as shibboleths, differentiating the elite from the rabble."

Children will learn their native language adequately whatever anyone does, and the attempt to teach them language is fraught with psychological perils. For example, to "correct" the way a child speaks is potentially to give him what used to be called an inferiority complex. Moreover, when schools undertake such correction they risk dividing the child from his parents and social milieu, for he will speak in one way and live in another, creating hostility and possibly rejection all around him. But happily, since every child is a linguistic genius, there is no need to do any such thing. Every child will have the linguistic equipment he needs, merely by virtue of growing older.

I need hardly point out that Pinker doesn't really believe anything of what he writes, at least if example is stronger evidence of belief than precept. Though artfully sown here and there with a demotic expression to prove that he is himself of the people, his own book is written, not surprisingly, in the kind of English that would please schoolmarms. I doubt very much whether it would have reached its twenty-fifth printing had he chosen to write it in the dialect of rural Louisiana, for example, or of the slums of Newcastle-upon-Tyne. Even had he chosen to do so, he might have found the writing rather difficult. I should like to see him try to translate a sentence from his book that I have taken at random—"The point that the argument misses is that although natural selection involves incremental steps that enhance functioning, the enhancements do not have to be an existing module"—into the language of the Glasgow or Detroit slums.

In fact Pinker has no difficulty in ascribing greater or lesser expressive virtues to languages and dialects. In attacking the idea that there are primitive languages, he quotes the linguist Joan Bresnan, who describes English as "a West Germanic language spoken in England and its former colonies" (no prizes for guessing the emotional connotations of this way of so describing it). Bresnan wrote an article comparing the use of the dative in English and Kivunjo, a language spoken on the slopes of Mount Kilimanjaro. Its use is much more complex in the latter language than in the former, making far more distinctions. Pinker comments: "Among the clever gadgets I have glimpsed in the grammars of so-called primitive groups, the complex Cherokee pronoun system seems especially handy. It distinguishes among 'you and I,' 'another person and I,' 'several other people and I,' and 'you, one or more other persons, and I,' which English crudely collapses into the all-purpose pronoun we." In other words, crudity and subtlety are concepts that apply between languages. And if so, there can be no real reason why they cannot apply within a language—why one man's usage should not be better, more expressive, subtler, than another's.

Similarly, Pinker attacks the idea that the English of the ghetto, Black English Vernacular, is in any way inferior to standard English. It is rule-governed like (almost) all other language. Moreover, "If the psychologists had listened to spontaneous conversations, they would have rediscovered the commonplace fact that American black culture is highly verbal; the subculture of street youths in particular is famous in the annals of anthropology for the value placed on linguistic virtuosity." But in appearing to endorse the idea of linguistic virtuosity, he is, whether he likes it or not, endorsing the idea of linguistic lack of virtuosity. And it surely requires very little reflection to come to the conclusion that Shakespeare had more linguistic virtuosity than, say, the average contemporary football player. Oddly enough, Pinker ends his encomium on Black English Vernacular with a schoolmarm's pursed lips: "The highest percentage of ungrammatical sentences [are to be] found in the proceedings of learned academic conferences."

Over and over again, Pinker stresses that children do not learn language by imitation; rather, they learn it because they are biologically predestined to do so. "Let us do away," he writes, with what one imagines to be a rhetorical sweep of his hand, "with the folklore that parents teach their children language." It comes as rather a surprise, then, to read the book's dedication: "For Harry and Roslyn Pinker, who gave me language."

Surely he cannot mean by this that they gave him language in the same sense as they gave him hemoglobin—that is to say, that they were merely the sine qua non of his biological existence as Steven Pinker. If so, why choose language of all the gifts that they gave him? Presumably he means that they gave him the opportunity to learn standard English, even if they did not speak it themselves.

It is utterly implausible to suggest that imitation of parents (or other social contacts) has nothing whatever to do with the acquisition of language. I hesitate to mention so obvious a consideration, but Chinese parents tend to have Chinese-speaking children, and Portuguese parents Portuguese-speaking ones. I find it difficult to believe that this is entirely a coincidence and that imitation has nothing to do with it. Moreover it is a sociological truism that children tend to speak not merely the language but the dialect of their parents.

Of course, they can escape it if they choose or need to do so: my mother, a native German speaker, arrived in England aged eighteen and learned to speak standard English without a trace of a German accent (which linguists say is a rare accomplishment) and without ever making a grammatical mistake. She didn't imitate her parents, perhaps, but she imitated someone. After her recent death I found her notebooks from 1939, in which she painstakingly practiced English, the errors growing fewer until there were none. I don't think she would have been favorably impressed by Professor Pinker's disdainful grammatical latitudinarianism—the latitudinarianism that, in British schools and universities, now extends not only to grammar but to spelling, as a friend of mine discovered recently.

A teacher in a state school gave his daughter a list of spellings to learn as homework, and my friend noticed that three out of ten of them were wrong. He went to the principal to complain, but she looked at the list and asked, "So what? You can tell what the words are supposed to mean." The test for her was not whether the spellings were correct but whether they were understandable. So much for the hobgoblins of contemporary schoolmarms.

The contrast between a felt and lived reality—in this case, Pinker's need to speak and write standard English because of its superior ability to express complex ideas—and the denial of it, perhaps in order to assert something original and striking, is characteristic of an intellectual climate in which the destruction of moral and social distinctions is proof of the very best intentions.

Pinker's grammatical latitudinarianism, when educationists like the principal of my friend's daughter's school take it seriously, has the practical effect of encouraging those born in the lower reaches of society to remain there, to enclose them in the mental world of their particular milieu. This is perfectly all right if you also believe that all stations in life are equally good and desirable and that there is nothing to be said for articulate reflection upon human existence. In other words, grammatical latitudinarianism is the natural ideological ally of moral and cultural relativism.

It so happens that I observed the importance of mastering standard, schoolmarmly grammatical speech in my own family. My father, born two years after his older brother, had the opportunity, denied his older brother for reasons of poverty, to continue his education. Accordingly my father learned to speak and write standard English, and I never heard him utter a single word that betrayed his origins. He could discourse philosophically without difficulty; I sometimes wished he had been a little less fluent.

My uncle, by contrast, remained trapped in the language of the slums. He was a highly intelligent man and, what is more, a very good one: he was one of those rare men, much less common than their opposite, from whom goodness radiated almost as a physical quality. No one ever met him without sensing his goodness of heart, his generosity of spirit.

But he was deeply inarticulate. His thoughts were too complex for the words and the syntax available to him. All through my childhood and beyond, I saw him struggle, like a man wrestling with an invisible boa constrictor, to express his far from foolish thoughts—thoughts of a complexity that my father expressed effortlessly. The frustration was evident on his face, though he never blamed anyone else for it. When, in Pinker's book, I read the transcript of an interview by the neuropsychologist Howard Gardner with a man who suffered from expressive dysphasia after a stroke—that is to say, an inability to articulate thoughts in language—I was, with great sadness, reminded of my uncle. Gardner asked the man about his job before he had a stroke.

> "I'm a sig . . . no . . . man . . . uh, well, . . . again." These words were emitted slowly, and with great effort. . . .
>
> "Let me help you," I interjected. "You were a signal . . ."
>
> "A sig-nal man . . . right," [he] completed my phrase triumphantly.
>
> "Were you in the Coast Guard?"
>
> "No, er, yes, yes . . . ship . . . Massachu . . . chusetts . . . Coast-guard . . . years."

It seemed to me that it was a cruel fate for such a man as my uncle not to have been taught the standard English that came to come so naturally to my father. As Montaigne tells us, there is no torture greater than that of a man who is unable to express what is in his soul.

Beginning in the 1950s, Basil Bernstein, a London University researcher, demonstrated the difference between the speech of middle- and working-class children, controlling for whatever it is that IQ measures. Working-class speech, tethered closely to the here and now, lacked the very aspects of standard English needed to express abstract or general ideas and to place personal experience in temporal or any other perspective. Thus, unless Pinker's despised schoolmarms were to take the working-class children in hand and deliberately teach them another speech code, they were doomed to remain where they were, at the bottom of a society that was itself much the poorer for not taking full advantage of their abilities, and that indeed would pay a steep penalty for not doing so. An intelligent man who can make no constructive use of his intelligence is likely to make a destructive, and self-destructive, use of it.

If anyone doubts that inarticulacy can be a problem, I recommend reading a report by the Joseph Rowntree Trust about British girls who get themselves pregnant in their teens (and sometimes their early teens) as an answer to their existential problems. The report is not in the least concerned with the linguistic deficiencies of these girls, but they are evident in the transcript in every reply to every question. Without exception, the girls had had a very painful experience of life and therefore much to express from hearts that must have been bursting. I give only one example, but it is representative. A girl, aged seventeen, explains why it is wonderful to have a baby:

> Maybe it's just—yeah, because maybe just—might be (um) it just feels great when—when like, you've got a child who just—you know—following you around, telling you they love you and I think that's—it's quite selfish, but that's one of the reasons why I became a mum because I wanted someone who'll—you know—love 'em to bits 'cos it's not just your child who's

the centre of your world, and that feels great as well, so I think—it's brilliant. It is fantastic because—you know—they're—the child's dependent on you and you know that (um)—that you—if you—you know—you've gotta do everything for the child and it just feels great to be depended on.

As I know from the experience of my patients, there is no reason to expect her powers of expression to increase spontaneously with age. Any complex abstractions that enter her mind will remain inchoate, almost a nuisance, like a fly buzzing in a bottle that it cannot escape. Her experience is opaque even to herself, a mere jumble from which it will be difficult or impossible to learn because, for linguistic reasons, she cannot put it into any kind of perspective or coherent order.

I am not of the ungenerous and empirically mistaken party that writes off such people as inherently incapable of anything better or as already having achieved so much that it is unnecessary to demand anything else of them on the grounds that they naturally have more in common with Shakespeare than with speechless animal creation. Nor, of course, would I want everyone to speak all the time in Johnsonian or Gibbonian periods. Not only would it be intolerably tedious, but much linguistic wealth would vanish. But everyone ought to have the opportunity to transcend the limitations of his linguistic environment, if it is a restricted one—which means that he ought to meet a few schoolmarms in his childhood. Everyone, save the handicapped, learns to run without being taught; but no child runs one hundred yards in nine seconds, or even fifteen seconds, without training. It is fatuous to expect that the most complex of human faculties, language, requires no special training to develop it to its highest possible power.

2006

What Makes
Dr. Johnson Great?

A FRIEND OF MINE, Russian by birth but English by adoption, who speaks English more elegantly and eloquently than most native speakers, once asked me of what, precisely, the greatness of Dr. Johnson consisted. He was asking only for information, in a spirit of inquiry; but the question took me aback, because the greatness of Dr. Johnson was something that I took for granted. If my friend had asked me to name a man whose greatness was his most salient characteristic, I think I would have named Dr. Johnson without a second thought.

"But," my friend continued, "Dr. Johnson was a writer, and the greatness of writers is in their writing. Who reads him now, or feels the need to do so?" He added that he had never read him but still considered himself well-read in English literature.

Johnson's quality of unreadness is not new and is equaled only by that of Walter Scott, whose once-famous historical romances are now read, I suspect, only rarely, and with a sinking heart and a sense of duty—even though *Ivanhoe* was allegedly Prime Minister Blair's favorite reading. Carlyle, in his essay on Boswell's *Life of Johnson*, says that the *Life* far exceeds in value anything Johnson wrote: "[A]lready, indeed," says Carlyle, "[Johnson's works] are becoming obsolete in this generation; and for some future generations may be valuable chiefly as Prolegomena and expository Scholia to this Johnsoniad of Boswell." This was written in 1832, less than half a century after Johnson's death, and as literary prophecy was not far from the mark. Boswell has many more readers than Johnson, and probably has had ever since Carlyle passed judgment.

Can a man be really great whose greatest claim to fame is to have been the subject of a great biography, perhaps the greatest ever written? Of the biographer himself, Macaulay wrote (one year before Carlyle): "Homer is not more decidedly the first of heroic poets, Shakespeare is not more decidedly the first of dramatists, Demosthenes is not more decidedly the first of orators, than Boswell is the first of biographers. He has no second. He has distanced all his competitors so decidedly that it is not worth while to place them." This despite the fact that the biography opens with the words, "To write the life of him who excelled all mankind in writing the lives of others . . . is an arduous, and may be reckoned in me a presumptuous task."

A great biography could be written, at least in theory, about a man who was not of the first importance. Johnson himself wrote a small biographical masterpiece about the reprobate poet Richard Savage, who would by now have been entirely forgotten had Johnson not done so. But great as Boswell's book is, it could not have been written about any man taken at random: Johnson found his Boswell, as the saying goes, but it would be truer to say that Boswell found his Johnson. By the end of the *Life*, most of us are convinced that the final encomium of the writer to his subject was fully justified: "Such was SAMUEL JOHNSON, a man whose talents, acquirements, and virtues were so extraordinary, that the more his character is considered, the more he will be regarded by the present age, and by posterity, with admiration and reverence."

My friend, who had read his Boswell and knew Johnson's witticisms well enough, persisted in denying that they were grounds for the unanimous conviction he found among educated speakers of English that Johnson deserves an honored place in the literary pantheon. We might love him for his peculiarities, esteem him for his character, admire him for his learning, wish we had been present to hear his repartee, yet none of this sufficiently accounts for our reverence for him. His *Dictionary* was no doubt a stupendous achievement, a colossal monument to individual industry and learning, but so was Alexander Cruden's concordance to the Bible, which provides cross-references for every single word in the King James version. Though Cruden's achievement was of the physical and mental magnitude of Johnson's *Dictionary*, we do not reverence him in the slightest. Cruden, in fact a very interesting man, is now almost forgotten.

I tried to convey to my friend my personal reaction to Johnson. When I look at Johnson's death mask, I think I see something of his tremendous character and intellect in the huge and craggy features, a rough nobility and a profundity of being, a face that bears the same proportion to the average human visage as the Himalayas do to the Cotswolds: but of course I recognize the objection that I find reflected there only what I was predisposed to find. Likewise when I look at Joshua Reynolds's portraits of Johnson: those extraordinary pictures by a painter who so loved and reverenced his subject and friend that he painted him precisely as he was—not graceful, not handsome, not elegant—convinced that his appearance would speak for itself, that of a man possessed of unmistakable force of character, an unceasing wrestler with the deepest problems of man's existence, a great soul. We may not always agree with Dr. Johnson's answers, but when we look at Reynolds's portraits of him, we can hardly doubt the sincerity, depth, and intelligence of his efforts. All the same, I had to admit (under the cross-examination of my friend) that great portraits are no guarantee of the greatness of their sitters.

Macaulay's summary of Boswell's biographical account gives us a clue as to why we are so moved by Johnson and tend to make him a touchstone of what we consider the most admirable, the highest type of man. Thanks to Boswell, says Macaulay, "Johnson grown old, Johnson in the fulness of his fame and in the enjoyment of a competent fortune, is better known to us than any other man in history." He continues:

> Every thing about him, his coat, his wig, his figure, his face, his scrofula, his St. Vitus's dance, his rolling walk, his blinking eye, the outward signs which too clearly marked his approbation of his dinner, his insatiable appetite for fish-sauce and veal-pie with plums, his inexhaustible thirst for tea, his trick of touching the posts as he walked, his mysterious practice of treasuring up scraps of orange-peel, his morning slumbers, his midnight disputations, his contortions, his mutterings, his gruntings, his puffings, his vigorous, acute and ready eloquence, his sarcastic wit, his vehemence, his insolence, his fits of tempestuous rage, his queer inmates, old Mr Levett and blind Mrs Williams [who lived for years in his household at his expense], the cat Hodge and the negro Frank are all as familiar to us as the objects by which we have been surrounded from childhood.

What Johnson said of the London of his time, that it contained all that human life can afford, seems also true of his own life. Johnson is a good but flawed man, always trying to be, but not always succeeding in being, a better one: he is proud, he is humble; he is weak, he is strong; he is prejudiced, he is generous-minded; he is tenderhearted, he is bad-tempered; he is foolish, he is wise; he is sure of himself, he is modest; he is idle, he is hardworking; he is opinionated, he is consumed by doubt; he is spiritual, he is carnal; he is hopeful, he is despairing; he is skeptical, he is credulous; he is melancholy, he is lighthearted; he is deferential, he is aware that he has no superior in the world; he is clumsy of body, he is elegant of mind and diction; he is a failure, he is triumphant. We never expect to meet anyone who, to such a degree, encompasses in his being all human vulnerability and human resilience.

Humility and pride contend in Johnson's heart and mind. He does not object in the slightest to social hierarchy—quite the contrary, and consistent with his profound conservatism, he repeatedly supports it as a necessary precondition of civilization—and he has no objection to inherited wealth, eminence, or influence. Yet when he feels slighted by a nobleman, he objects to the insult to his own worth in the most manly, uncompromising, eloquent, and fearless fashion. Writing to Lord Chesterfield, who encouraged him at first to compile his great *Dictionary*, then ignored him entirely during his years of almost superhuman toil, and finally tried to pose as his great patron once he had brought his *Dictionary* to completion, Johnson says in prose whose nobility rings down the centuries: "Is not a Patron, my Lord, one who looks with unconcern on a man struggling for life in the water, and, when he has reached ground, encumbers him with help? . . . I hope it is no very cynical asperity, not to confess obligations where no benefit has been received, or to be unwilling that the Publick should consider me as owing that to a Patron, which Providence has enabled me to do for myself."

His integrity (a virtue no more common in his time than now) shines out from a letter that he wrote to a lady who had asked him to recommend her son to the archbishop of Canterbury for admission to a university (either Oxford or Cambridge):

MADAM,

I hope you will believe that my delay in answering your letter could proceed only from my unwillingness to destroy any hope that you had formed. Hope is itself a species of happiness, and, perhaps, the chief happiness which this world affords; but, like all other pleasures immoderately enjoyed, the excesses of hope must be expiated by pain. . . . When you made your request to me, you should have considered, Madam, what you were asking. You ask me to solicit a great man, to whom I never spoke, for a young person whom I had never seen, upon a supposition which I had no means of knowing to be true.

I don't think you could read this letter without perceiving in its writer great intellect, eloquence, wit, knowledge of life derived from deep reflection upon experience, and—what perhaps most compels respect—moral seriousness.

Some people might (and did) find Johnson sententious. His precepts roll through our minds like thunder through hills and valleys—but do they have more meaning than thunder has? They often appear obvious, but they are obvious not because they are clichés or truisms or things that everyone knows and has always known, nor are they like the sermons of a jobbing clergyman who goes through the motions of extolling virtue and condemning sin because it is his job to do so. Johnson's precepts are obvious because they are distillations of the lessons of common human experience, and, once expressed, they are impossible to deny.

At every moment Johnson reflects on the moral meaning and consequences of human life. In his biography of the dissolute poet and his sometime friend Richard Savage, written at an early stage of his career and originally published anonymously, Johnson exhibits both compassion for, and clear-sighted acknowledgment of the faults of, his subject, whose life he treats as an object for moral and psychological reflection. Who could fail to recognize a common human pattern in his delineation of Savage's greatest failing?

> By imputing none of his miseries to himself he continued to act upon the same principles and to follow the same path; was never made wiser by his sufferings, nor preserved by one misfortune from falling into another. He proceeded throughout his life to tread the same steps on the same circle; always applauding his past conduct, or at least forgetting it, to amuse himself

with phantoms of happiness which were dancing before him, and willingly turned his eye from the light of reason, when it would have discovered the illusion and shewn him, what he never wanted to see, his real state.

The necessity for honest self-examination, if avoidable misery is to be avoided, could hardly be more eloquently expressed; and it is one of the most serious defects of modern culture and the welfare state that they discourage such self-examination by encouraging the imputation of all miseries to others, and they thus have a disastrous effect upon human character.

Johnson was a man of the Enlightenment. He had a great interest in the experimental sciences, for example, and placed a high value on reason. But he was also acutely aware of the limits of the Enlightenment. He could hold irreconcilable dilemmas in his mind without giving way to nihilism or irrationalism. He was profoundly anti-Romantic: his *Life of Savage* ends with an implicit denunciation of the Romantic notion that the possession of talent excuses a man from the demands of the moral life or social existence:

> This relation [the biography] will not be wholly without its use if . . . those who, in confidence of superior capacities or attainments, disregard the common maxims of life, shall be reminded that nothing will supply the want of prudence, and that negligence and irregularity long continued will make knowledge useless, wit ridiculous, and genius contemptible.

No one could accuse Johnson of being a mindless conformist; it is doubtful whether a more individual individual has ever existed; but he was always prepared to place that limit on his own appetites that, in the opinion of his acquaintance, Edmund Burke, qualified a man for freedom.

In his censure of disregard for the common maxims of life, Johnson displays his deep though flexible conservatism, a conservatism not of the mulish kind opposed to all possible change

(Johnson invariably praises advances in knowledge and industry, for example), but of the kind that believes that most men, instead of reasoning from first principles on all occasions, need the aid of the accumulated wisdom of custom, precept, and prejudice most of the time if they are to live a moral life in reasonable harmony and happiness with one another. Johnson criticizes Dean Swift, in his brief biography of him, for his willful and self-conscious eccentricity. "Singularity," he says, "as it implies a contempt of the general practice, is a kind of defiance which justly provokes the hostility of ridicule; he, therefore, who indulges in peculiar traits, is worse than others, if he be not better." Note that Johnson does not deny the possibility of betterment, nor does he believe that the best path has always been found already. But he denies that deviation from the common path, for reasons of vanity, is a virtue; on the contrary, it is a vice. We might have had fewer social problems today if this view had had more currency.

A comparison of Johnson's *Rasselas* with Voltaire's *Candide*—by common consent the two greatest philosophical tales ever written—makes Johnson's greatness stand forth in sharp relief. Published in the same year, 1759, both works attacked facile optimism about human existence. By strange coincidence, both authors had written long poems that addressed the question of optimism before they wrote these two tales exploring the same subject. Johnson's "The Vanity of Human Wishes" suggests that lasting happiness is not of this world, whether sought in power, wealth, or knowledge. Bitterness and disappointment are even the scholar's lot:

> There mark what Ills the Scholar's Life assail,
> Toil, Envy, Want, the Garret, and the Jail.
> See Nations slowly wise and meanly just,
> To buried Merit raise the tardy Bust.

For Johnson, no form of life is free of care; each has pains at least equal to its joys.

After the Lisbon earthquake of 1755, which killed thirty thousand and left the city in ruins, Voltaire wrote a poem that questioned the Leibnizian notion, expressed most pithily in Pope's famous words, "Whatever is, is right." Divine Providence being benign, this notion holds, all must be for the best in this, the best of all possible worlds, despite appearances to the contrary, and nothing could be other than it is. Voltaire sharply challenged this view in his "Poem on the Lisbon Disaster; Or an Examination of the Axiom that All Is Well."

> Will you say, on seeing this pile of dead:
> "God is revenged, their death is the price of their crimes"?
> What crime, what fault, have these infants committed
> Who are crushed and bloody on their mother's breast?
> Did Lisbon, which is no more, have more vices
> Than Paris, than London, which are sunk in pleasures?

Voltaire's *Candide*, which has always had more renown than Johnson's *Rasselas*, is nevertheless far the more superficial work, its irony crude and shallow compared with that of *Rasselas*. The surface similarities of the stories only underline their difference in depth. The one, *Candide*, attacks a philosophical doctrine; the other, *Rasselas*, addresses a human condition that is with us still. Portraits of the two authors reveal the difference in their character: Voltaire looks like an unregenerate cynic who wants to shock the world by sneering at it, while Johnson looks like a man determined to penetrate to the heart of human existence. The more serious man is also far the funnier.

Candide, a naive, good-natured young man, lives happily in a Westphalian *schloss*, the home of Baron Thunder-ten-tronckh. He falls under the philosophical spell of the household tutor, Dr. Pangloss, who believes that "all is for the best in this, the best of all possible worlds." The book traces Candide's subsequent wanderings round the globe, in the course of which he suffers horrible injustices and ill-treatment, as do all his acquaintances.

He witnesses arbitrary misfortunes, including the Lisbon earthquake. In the end, he and Dr. Pangloss are reunited on the banks of the Bosphorus, where they find some kind of tranquillity and happiness. Pangloss, absurdly, still maintains his optimism: since "all events are linked together in the best of all possible worlds," for him their current happiness is the happy consequence of all that they had hitherto suffered and witnessed. Pangloss having been hanged and nearly burned alive by the Inquisition (among many other horrors), the absurdity of his doctrine is evident.

Rasselas is a prince of Abyssinia who, like all royal Abyssinian princes, lives in "the happy valley" until the time comes for him to ascend the throne. (Interestingly, while Voltaire, the rationalist and universalist, displays considerable contempt for German culture, the patriotic and more locally rooted Johnson shows no contempt whatever for Abyssinian or Egyptian culture, suggesting that rootedness and imaginative sympathy for others are not incompatible.) In the happy valley, Rasselas has all his wants supplied; he lives in luxury among ample and continual amusements, and yet he feels discontent despite the perfection of the place and the ease of his existence.

He and his sister, Nekayah, and a philosophical tutor, Imlac, leave the happy valley and search the world for the right way to live. Imlac acts as a kind of ironical chorus to the ideas of the prince and princess. On their journey they meet the powerful and the powerless, the hermit, the socialite, the sage, the ignoramus, the sophisticate, the peasant: all modes of life, even the most outwardly attractive, have drawbacks, and none answers to all human desires or is free of anxieties and miseries. In the end, the royal pair realize that of the "wishes that they had formed . . . none could be obtained."

The difference in depth of the two books is readily apparent from the difference in the irony that each author employs. Voltaire is heavy and obvious; Johnson, despite his stylistic orotundity, is light and subtle. Candide is expelled from his happy home, Rasselas wants to escape his: already a great difference in depth, for Candide's misfortunes eventuate from outside himself, while Rasselas experiences Man's existential, internally generated dissatisfaction and restlessness. Since no one could possibly imagine a place better than the happy valley, Johnson confronts us from the first with man's inability ever to be satisfied with what he has, which, he suggests, is his glory but also his misery.

Here is Voltaire on Baron Thunder-ten-tronckh: "Monsieur the Baron was one of the most powerful lords in Westphalia, for his château had a door and some windows." Yes, Germany was backward at the time, but the satire is heavy-handed. And the objects of Voltaire's satire are similarly unsubtle. Here is the account of the aftermath of the battle between the Bulgars and the Abars in their war about nothing (*Candide* was written during the Seven Years' War):

> At last, while the two kings had Te Deums sung, each in his own camp, Candide took the opportunity to reason on causes and effects. He passed over piles of dead and dying, and first reached a nearby village; it was in ashes; it was an Abar village that the Bulgars had burnt, according to public law. Here badly wounded old men watched their wives die of slit throats, who held their children to their bloody breasts; there, young girls, slit open after having assuaged the natural needs of several heroes, sighed their last; others, half-burnt, begged that they should be killed off. Brains were spread on the ground, beside cut-off arms and legs.

And here is Voltaire's description of the Portuguese reaction to the earthquake of 1755, which Candide and Pangloss witnessed immediately upon their arrival in Lisbon:

> After the earthquake that had destroyed three-quarters of Lisbon, the learned men of the country had not found a more

effective means of preventing total ruin than that of giving the people a good auto-da-fé; it was decided by the University of Coimbra that the spectacle of several people being burnt slowly was an infallible preventative of earthquakes.

This is quite funny, and of course the horrors of war and the excesses of superstition are suitable, if easy, targets of criticism. But there is something irredeemably adolescent in Voltaire's satire, which also lacks real, nonabstract feeling for humanity. Baron Grimm noticed this when the book first came out: a judicious critic writing two thousand years from now, he said, will probably say that the author was only twenty-five when he wrote it. In fact, Voltaire was sixty-five, fifteen years older than Johnson.

When we turn to Johnson, we find a mind of a completely different quality. Repeatedly we marvel at Johnson's wisdom and maturity. Rasselas falls for a time under the spell of a rhetorician in Cairo who extols the control of the passions and emotions. In a chapter titled "The Prince Finds a Wise and Happy Man," he listens to the rhetorician give a lecture:

> His look was venerable, his action graceful, his pronunciation clear, and his diction elegant. He shewed . . . that human nature is degraded and debased, when the lower faculties predominate over the higher; that when fancy, the parent of passion, usurps the dominion of the mind, nothing ensues but the natural effect of unlawful government, perturbation and confusion.

Rasselas "listened to him with the veneration due to the instructions of a superior being" and visited him the following day to learn more wisdom from him. But "he found the philosopher in a room half darkened, and his eyes misty, and his face pale."

The philosopher's only daughter has died in the night of a fever. "What I suffer cannot be remedied, what I have lost cannot be supplied." Rasselas then confronts him with his own fine words about the primacy of reason over sentiments, to which the philosopher replies that Rasselas speaks like one who has never lost anyone. "What comfort," asks the philosopher, "can truth and reason afford me? Of what effect are they now, but to tell me that my daughter will not be restored?"

Rasselas, "whose humanity would not suffer him to insult misery with reproof, went away convinced of the emptiness of rhetorical sound, and the inefficacy of polished periods and studied sentences."

Here is real education of both the heart and mind—and confirmation of Imlac's warning to Rasselas to "be not too hasty . . . to trust or to admire the teachers of morality: they discourse like angels, but they live like men." The prince is a callow, young, inexperienced man, yet he is good enough of heart to understand at once that sometimes fellow-feeling must trump logic and argument. And Johnson's profundity is to know that reason's evident limitations do not make it—or even rhetoric's "polished periods and studied sentences"—valueless, but only limited. Our capacity of reason is magnificent, to be sure; but there are mysteries in human experience that transcend even reason's explanatory powers.

In a later episode, Rasselas and his sister discuss the advantages and disadvantages of early and late marriage, and come to the conclusion that there is no means by which the advantages of both can be reconciled and the disadvantages be avoided. All the things that men desire are not compatible, and therefore discontent is the lot of Man; as Rasselas's sister, Nekayah, puts it: "No man can, at the same time, fill his cup from the source and from the mouth of the Nile." A man who understands this will not as a result cease to experience incompatible desires—for example, those for security and excitement—but he will be less embittered that he cannot have everything he wants. An understanding of the imperfectibility of life is necessary for both happiness and virtue.

Throughout his writings, Johnson says things that strike us as obvious—but with the force of revelation. What he says of Richard Savage is, in fact, far truer of himself: "[W]hat no other man would have thought on, it now appears scarcely possible for any man to miss." His writings appeal to "whoever will attend to the motions of his own mind," attention that for him is a fundamental duty. Few men have ever paid more serious attention to introspection than Dr. Johnson, not as a means of self-indulgence but as necessary to moral improvement and to an understanding of human nature. "We all know our own state," he says elsewhere, "if we could be induced to consider it." It is Dr. Johnson's purpose to recall us to ourselves: perhaps that explains why people now find him so disturbing to read.

He says things that are obvious, but only obvious once he has pointed them out. In *The Rambler*, number 159, for example, he tells us that bashfulness is often a disguised self-importance. The bashful person "considers that what he shall say or do will never be forgotten; that renown or infamy are suspended upon every syllable." But, says Johnson, "He that considers how little he dwells upon the condition of others, will learn how little the attention of others is attracted by himself."

Every chapter of *Rasselas* contains thoughts so penetrating that they could only be those of a man of the character portrayed by Boswell. Johnson is brandy to Voltaire's thin beer (a strange reversal of national comestibles). Take the visit of Rasselas and Imlac to the Pyramids. When Imlac proposes the trip, Rasselas objects that it is men, not their past works, that interest him. Imlac replies: "To judge rightly of the present we must oppose it to the past; for all judgement is comparative, and of the future nothing can be known." Having established that "to see men we must see their works," Imlac continues: "If we act only for ourselves, to neglect the study of history is not prudent; if we are entrusted with the care of others, it is not just."

When they finally arrive at the Pyramids, Imlac's reflections are profound:

> [F]or the pyramids, no reason has ever been given adequate to the cost and labour of the work. The narrowness of the chambers proves that it could afford no retreat from enemies, and treasures might have been reposited at far less expense with equal security. It seems to have been erected only in compliance with that hunger of imagination which preys incessantly upon life, and must be always appeased by some employment. Those who have already all that they can enjoy must enlarge their desires. He that has built for use till use is supplied must begin to build for vanity.

And finally:

> I consider this mighty structure as a monument of the insufficiency of human enjoyments.

The last chapter of the book is titled "The Conclusion, in which Nothing Is Concluded." This is not a facile irony, as it might have been if a postmodernist had written it; it is a statement of the difficulties with which Johnson wrestled all his life—as we all must, if we pause for thought.

When one considers that Voltaire was no inconsiderable person and yet was shallow by comparison with Johnson, and that Johnson wrote *Rasselas* in a week to pay for his mother's medical treatment and funeral, one begins to grasp the intellectual and moral dimension of the man. What a mighty mind, so furnished that it could write such a book in a week, to pay such comparatively trifling bills! Of course the speed of his work also explains why Johnson was always aware, and felt deeply guilty, that he had not achieved as much as he might had he applied himself more diligently, and that "I have neither attempted nor formed any scheme of Life by which I may do good and please God" (this on his sixty-second birthday). Johnson was never satisfied with himself and did not blame the world for his dissatisfaction; fifty years after he was cheekily disobliging to his impoverished father, the GREAT SAMUEL JOHNSON, in Boswell's phrase, stood bareheaded for an hour in the rain in Uttoxeter marketplace in atonement for his sin.

Johnson is an unusual writer, in that he is far greater than the sum of his parts. For all the excellence of *Rasselas*, Johnson is not among the greatest imaginative writers of English literature; only a few lines of his poetry are now remembered; his essays, though vastly more self-analytically honest and morally useful than anything Freud wrote, do not appeal to an age that prefers psychobabble to true reflection, and in which self-exculpation is de rigueur.

But, his *Dictionary*—43,000 definitions and 110,000 citations from literature, a work of near-unimaginable proportions when one considers the labor of devising for oneself the definition of even one word—provides a key to his abiding greatness. His definition of the word "conscience" is "the knowledge or faculty by which we judge the goodness or wickedness of ourselves." Above all, Johnson saw the exercise of judgment as the supreme human duty; however inviting it is for human beings to avoid judgment, because it is impossible to judge correctly of everything, it is inescapably necessary to make judgments. Truly, he was as Boswell described him, a man whose extraordinary "character" compels "admiration and reverence"—and illuminates every line he wrote. "His mind resembled the vast amphitheatre, the Coliseum of Rome," Boswell wrote. "In the centre stood his judgement, which like a mighty gladiator, combated those apprehensions that, like the wild beasts of the arena, were all around in cells, ready to be let out upon him." And, of course, upon us.

I think I can return an answer to my once-Russian friend.

2006

Truth vs. Theory

THERE ARE TWO William Shakespeares. The first is the man born in Stratford, who never seemed to spell his name the same way twice, who was deeply interested in minor financial transactions and the accumulation of property, and who left his wife his second-best bed; the other is the man who left the world the greatest literary legacy ever known. A considerable body of scholarship, the work principally of enthusiastic and learned amateurs, seeks to establish that William Shakespeare in the first sense was not William Shakespeare in the second sense.

I do not wish to enter this controversy, in part because of sheer cowardice. The convinced Baconians, Oxfordians, and Marlovians—those who believe that Francis Bacon, Edward de Vere, and Christopher Marlowe were the true authors of those plays and poems ascribed to Shakespeare—have usually come to their conclusions by means of minute and painstaking, even obsessive, scholarship, using every technique from textual and historical analysis to cryptography and numerology. They do not take kindly to the casual denigration of their efforts by people who assume without further ado that the two Shakespeares were one and the same man.

But, one argument in the controversy interests me, common to all those who oppose the Stratfordians (as the Baconians, Oxfordians, and Marlovians somewhat derisively call those who believe that the two Shakespeares were one): that the plays' author was so understanding of every aspect of human nature, and so intimately knowledgeable about so many fields of human endeavor—as well as about all the strata of the society in which he lived, including the highest—that he could not have been a mere grammar-school boy from Stratford. The author must have had much more formal education than that.

Many books have over the years commented on Shakespeare's knowledge of soldiering, sailing and navigation, the law, and so forth; and I have accumulated a small library of books, both British and American, written over the last century and a half, by doctors commenting on Shakespeare's medical knowledge.

For the most part, these volumes are compilations of every conceivable medical reference in Shakespeare, arranged by play, by disease, or by relevant medical specialty. They include Ernest Jones's famous—or perhaps "notorious" would be a better word—analysis of Hamlet's Oedipus complex, and a much more recent volume on Shakespeare and neurobiology. The general tone is respectful astonishment at the accuracy of many of Shakespeare's medical observations.

No medical author, as far as I know, has suggested as a consequence that Shakespeare must have had medical training, though many have suggested that he might have picked up medical knowledge from his son-in-law, a university-trained physician. His name was Dr. John Hall: he held a degree from Cambridge and probably had studied on the continent as well. But, Hall settled in Stratford only in 1600 and married Shakespeare's daughter, Susanna, in 1608. By then, of course, Shakespeare had written most of his plays and made most of his medical observations and allusions: Hall, therefore, could not have been the chief source of his medical knowledge.

Even so, it is instructive to compare Shakespeare's and Hall's medical observations. For Shakespeare I could choose from many cases, but one will suffice. Here is Falstaff's death, as described by Mistress Quickly in *Henry V*:

'A made a finer end and went away an it had been any christom child; 'a parted even just between twelve and one, even at the turning o' the tide: for after I saw him fumble with the sheets and play with flowers and smile upon his fingers' ends, I knew there was but one way; for his nose was as sharp as a pen, and 'a babbled of green fields. "How now, Sir John!" quoth I; "What, man! Be o' good cheer." So 'a cried out "God, God, God!" three or four times. Now I, to comfort him, bid him 'a should not think of God; I hoped there was no need to trouble himself with any such thoughts yet. So 'a bade me lay more clothes on his feet: I put my hand into the bed and felt them, and they were as cold as any stone; then I felt to his knees, and they were as cold as any stone, and so upward and upward, and all was as cold as any stone.

One of the merits of this passage—and it is characteristic of Shakespeare that the merits of his writing should be so multiform, combining in equal measure truth, humanity, tolerance, wisdom, understanding, love, irony, and poetry—is its beautiful and accurate description of delirium. Here are some of the diagnostic criteria for delirium in the World Health Organization's International Classification of Diseases:

> (i) impairment of consciousness [with] reduced ability to direct, focus, sustain, and shift attention;
> (ii) global disturbance of cognition [with] perceptual distortions, illusions and hallucinations, most often visual; impairment of abstract thinking and comprehension . . . typically with some degree of incoherence;
> (iii) psychomotor disturbances [with] hypo- or hyperactivity and unpredictable shifts from one to the other;
> (iv) emotional disturbances, e.g., depression, anxiety or fear, irritability, euphoria, apathy or . . . perplexity.

Mistress Quickly, then, was a fine observer. Furthermore, the "nose as sharp as a pen" is a most precise and correct observation of a man in his death throes.

Now let us turn to Dr. Hall, whose medical observations, compiled from his notes after his death, appeared as a book, *Select Observations on English Bodies of Eminent Persons in Desperate Diseases*, that went through three editions in the seventeenth century. It is to go from the sublime to what, from our current standpoint, appears to be the ridiculous. I take a case at random: all eighty-two in the book are of the same intellectual ilk.

> Mr John Trap (Minister, for his piety and learning second to none) about the 33 year of his age, of a melancholy temper, and by much Study fell into Hypochondriac Melancholy, and pain of the Spleen, with some Scorbutic Symptoms, viz. Difficulty of breathing after gentle motion of the Body, beating of the Heart, with fainting at the rising of the Vapours, and became a little better when they were dispersed. He had a gentle Erratic fever, so that he was much amaciated; after he had done preaching on the Sabbath, he could scarce speak; his Urine changed often, his pulse was mutable and unequal, and he languished much. Some ordinary medicines were used, but not succeeding, he desired my help and counsel, which was readily performed by me in prescribing the following, by which he was restored from the very jaws of Death, both safely, quickly and pleasantly.

Among the prescriptions, not all of them pleasant, were: tartar vitriolatus (potassium sulphate) and mercurius dulcis (mercurous chloride), both given in boiled apple pap; cream of tartar; chalybeate wine; pectoral rolls (containing maiden hair and hyssop); sceletyrs syrup; raisins dried in the sun, boiled in a sack to the consistency of a paste, passed through a strainer and mixed with conserve of rosemary flowers and bugloss; citron pills; cinnamon; saffron; anti-scorbutic beer; solution of water snails; solution of frogs' spawn; and emetic infusion.

Apparently Trap recovered, partly, no doubt, from fear of further treatment by Hall. The doctor had many worse things up his therapeutic sleeve, such as goose, peacock, pigeon, and hen dung; ox bile; spiders' webs; and oil of scorpions.

This seemingly eclectic farrago of prescriptions found its basis, if somewhat distantly, in the Galenical theory of humors. There were four such humors, each partaking of one of the qualities of the four elements of Greek philosophy. Blood was airy, which is to say warm and moist; phlegm was watery, that is, cold and moist; yellow bile was fiery (hot and dry); and black bile was earthy (cold and dry). Every person had his distinct temperament, according to the predominance of the humors within him, whether sanguine, phlegmatic, choleric, or melancholic; illness was the upset of the balance between the humors. The purpose of medical treatment was to restore that balance, and medicines either promoted the deficient humor or tempered the excessive one. Oil of earthworms, for example, exerted a cooling and moisturizing effect, useful in treating those illnesses that excessive yellow bile had supposedly caused.

The Galenical theory was an article of uncritical faith for university-trained physicians. Training consisted of indoctrination, memorization, and regurgitation. No deviation was permissible, and even refinement or elaboration was hazardous. Outright challenge was professionally dangerous. The theory therefore took many centuries to overthrow; mastery of it, and the treatments it entailed, distinguished real physicians from mere empirics and quacks. Hall saw his patients through Galenical eyes; he was the master of an all-sufficient theory that made close observation of them redundant, indeed *infra dignitatum.* That is why it is almost impossible now to diagnose anything from his descriptions of his patients. He didn't need to observe: he had his theory, and so he knew everything in advance.

His book, incidentally, records only his successes. They confirmed that his theory was right all along, otherwise—does it not follow?—they would not have been successes.

Shakespeare was, of course, conversant with Galen's theory of humors. This no more means that he must have had university training in medicine than that a modern man who has heard of the germ theory of disease must be a microbiologist. But

Shakespeare was not in thrall to Galenism as was his son-in-law: in other words, it was precisely his lack of university training that permitted him to be so acute an observer. While he needed a sophisticated basic education to be Shakespeare, the author of the plays, university training, at least with regard to medicine, would have diminished rather than enhanced his work. A contemporary medical man can learn something from Shakespeare; he can learn nothing from Hall. As Orwell pointed out, it takes effort and determination to see what is in front of one's face. Among the efforts required is the discarding of the lenses of excessive or bogus theorizing. When it comes to our attempts to understand the phenomena of our own society, I cannot help but wonder how many of us are in the grip of theories that are the equivalent of Hall's Galenical theory, and whether as a result we do not prescribe the legislative equivalents of human skull, mummy dust, and jaw of pike.

As to why people adopt theories that conflict with the most minimal honest reflection, I will quote T. S. Eliot, who, while not always right, was right about this:

> Half the harm that is done in the world is due to people who want to feel important. They don't want to do harm—but the harm does not interest them . . . or they do not see it . . . because they are absorbed in the endless struggle to think well of themselves.

Eliot might have added: the endless struggle to look well in the eyes of their fellow intellectuals and the fear of losing caste. But as a result of their efforts, as Orwell also famously said, "We have sunk to a depth in which re-statement of the obvious is the first duty of intelligent men."

2005

A Drinker of Infinity

◈ SOMEONE who had known Arthur Koestler told me a little story about him. Koestler was playing Scrabble with his wife, and he put the word "vince" down on the board.

"Arthur," said his wife, "what does 'vince' mean?"

Koestler, who never lost his strong Hungarian accent but whose mastery of English was such that he was undoubtedly one of the twentieth century's great prose writers in the language, replied (one can just imagine with what light in his eyes): "To vince is to flinch slightly viz pain."

How many people could define a word in their first language with such elegant precision, let alone in their fourth, and moreover combine it with such irresistibly wicked humor? One can see in this trifling incident how being with anyone less brilliant than Arthur Koestler must have seemed intolerably dull to any woman who had been in love with him.

As it happens, Koestler's relations with women now have more to do with his reputation than does anything he ever wrote. Since the 1998 publication of David Cesarani's biographical study, Koestler's name has been synonymous with rape, possibly serial in nature, and the abuse of women. I tested this association on several friends with literary interests: though none had read Cesarani's book, in each case the first thought on hearing Koestler's name was of rape. It is doubtful whether any biography has ever affected the reputation of an author more profoundly than did Cesarani's; and its effect is proof, if we needed any, that books have an influence far beyond their actual readership.

Cesarani is a serious scholar, not a man to manufacture sensational claims for nonscholarly purposes; and in fact his widely publicized revelations, which came as a considerable shock, receive a kind of confirmation from a scene in Koestler's novel *Arrival and Departure*, published in 1943.

The book is at least partly autobiographical. Its protagonist (hero would be too positive a word) is Peter Slavek, a young refugee and former Communist militant from an unnamed Balkan country now under Nazi occupation. Slavek arrives in the capital of a neutral country—clearly Lisbon, Portugal—from which he hopes to reach England and enlist in the British forces, the only ones still fighting the Nazis at that time. Koestler himself reached England from Portugal with the same idea in mind, and his description of Lisbon's wartime atmosphere clearly draws on firsthand experience.

While in Lisbon, Slavek falls in love with, or forms an infatuation for, Odette, a young French refugee awaiting a visa for America. Odette has taken no notice of Slavek, but one day she visits a friend's apartment where the Balkan refugee is temporarily staying. The friend is absent, so Slavek and Odette are alone. There follows a scene that suggests that Koestler was as personally acquainted with rape as he was with the fervid atmosphere of wartime Lisbon.

Slavek declares his love for Odette; she rejects him and prepares to leave. "He jerked himself to his feet, reached the door almost in one jump and got hold of her as she was passing into the hall," Koestler writes. Then the author says of Slavek that he was doing what several rapists have told me that they sought to do—*protect* their victims: "As if the door were a death-trap and she were in danger of falling into it, [he] pressed her against him with a protecting gesture, while with his foot he kicked the door shut." Odette struggles, but "her very struggling," Koestler writes, makes Slavek's grip "close tighter around her, like the noose of a trap"—not the activity of an agent but the operation of a mechanical contrivance.

The situation calms a little, and Slavek realizes that he should have let his arms drop with embarrassment, but then "she began struggling again in renewed fury, and this automatically made him tighten his grip." Koestler describes Slavek as more terrified than Odette.

Then comes the actual rape:

> She struggled breathlessly, hammering her fists against his breast. . . . God, how unreasonable she was. . . . All he wanted was to make her understand that he didn't want anything from her. . . . By her furious struggling she caused him to press her back, step by step, from the door. His lips babbled senseless words that were meant to calm; but now it was too late, the flames leapt up, enveloping him. . . . With blind eyes he fell as they stumbled against a couch . . . [and he] rammed his knee against her legs, felt them give way and a second later her whole body go limp.

After it is all over, Odette cries. Slavek takes her hand, and feels encouraged when she does not withdraw it to explain and justify his actions: "You know, I am not so sure that you will always regret it, although for the moment you are still angry with me." Then he contrives to blur the distinction between voluntary and coerced sexual relations: "Nowadays things often start this way, the end at the beginning I mean. In the old days people had to wait years before they were allowed to go to bed and then found out that they didn't really like each other, it had all been a mirage of their glands. If you start the other way round you won't need to find out whether you really care."

Odette's reply absolves Slavek of any need to feel remorse: "The whole point is that if you knock a woman about for long enough and get on her nerves and wear her down, there comes a moment when she suddenly feels how silly all this struggling and kicking is, so much ado about nothing." Sexual intercourse, then, has no more moral significance than urination or any other physiological function. "You probably think what an irresistible seducer you are, while in fact all you did was get her to this zero level where she says—after all, why not?" And to confirm the Slavek-Odette-Koestler theory, Slavek and Odette go on to have a short and intense love affair.

Koestler's description of a rape seems to be from the inside; and if Cesarani is right, it gives us the very model of Koestler's conduct and experience. He might even have suffered from (if "suffered from" is quite the right phrase) what psychiatrists call "coercive paraphilia": sexual excitement brought on by the act of physical subjugation, a pompous name sometimes being the nearest that medical science can come to an explanation. Slavek's argument, of course, is virtually a rapist's charter. But the uncomfortable fact is that some of the women whom Koestler abused remained friends with him for the rest of their lives. It would take an entire book fully to explore all the evasions in the passage I have quoted, as well as the social and psychological questions it raises.

There is much more to Koestler, of course, than sexual perversity, even if it is difficult nowadays to read anything that he wrote without first donning rape-tinted spectacles. *Arrival and Departure* is not just about Slavek's love life: it passionately engages with the most important political questions of the day.

For example, the book gave the most graphic description until then published of the gassing of the Jews in Eastern Europe, not as isolated massacres but as part of a deliberate genocidal policy; and it drew an explicit comparison—now banal and commonplace, but then brave and arresting—between Hitler and Stalin, pointing out their similarities, despite their enmity. Meeting an intelligent Nazi agent called Bernard, Slavek asks

him why the Nazis, so anti-Communist, nevertheless copied Soviet methods "to a considerable extent." Bernard replies:

> There is of course a certain affinity between your ex-fatherland
> and ours. Both are governed by authoritarian state bureaucra-
> cies on a collectivist basis; both are streamlined police states
> run by economic planning, the one-party system and scientific
> terror. . . . It is a phase of history as inevitable as was the
> spreading of the feudal, and later of the capitalist, system. Our
> two countries are merely the forerunners of the post-individu-
> alist, post-liberal era.

To have written this passage at a time when books praising
our gallant Soviet allies poured forth from the press—when even
conservatives, always very few among the intelligentsia, had replaced their visceral hatred of the Soviet Union with admiration—
was an act of considerable courage.

Koestler's reputation as a writer had declined well before
Cesarani's revelations. He had become an author of the kind
one encounters during late adolescence or early adulthood,
whom one catches like the literary equivalent of glandular fever,
but to whom, once read, one develops a lifelong immunity.
Once one of the world's most famous authors, he became as
dated as the youthful fashions of three decades ago.

There were several reasons for this. By 1980, if not before, the
burning political issues of his early adulthood—communism, the
rise of fascism, and the establishment of a Zionist state—were of
less concern to new generations of readers. Many regarded
Koestler's subsequent obsessions—Indian mysticism, Lamarckian
biology, nonreductionist science, and parapsychology—as bizarre
or even dotty, the symptoms of a mind that had lost its way. In
his will he endowed a chair in parapsychology at Edinburgh University. He regarded telepathy and precognition as established
facts, largely because of the now-discredited experiments of
J. B. Rhine at Duke University. He began to collect examples of

startling coincidences, as if they could tell us something about noncausal relations between events. Like Sir Arthur Conan Doyle before him, he seemed to the public to have traveled from serious authorship to spiritualist crankdom.

The penultimate nail in the coffin of his reputation, before Cesarani's revelations, was his double suicide with his wife, who was twenty years younger, in 1983. While he had both severe Parkinson's disease (causing a decline in his mental powers) and leukemia (from which he was soon to die, in any case), his wife, who swallowed a fatal dose of barbiturates with him, was in perfect health. Many believed—without adequate evidence—that Koestler had bullied his wife into ending her life with him.

This was the second double suicide of a great Central European writer of adopted British citizenship and his wife, the first being that of Stefan and Lotte Zweig. But whereas Zweig killed himself in despair at the state of the world, Koestler killed himself in despair at the state of his health—no doubt a commentary on the direction, not wholly bad, in which the world had moved in the intervening forty years. But it suggested great egotism and cast doubt on the sincerity, or at least disinterestedness, of all Koestler's previous commitments.

Koestler does not deserve such summary dismissal, for if any figure could claim to have encapsulated in his own life—and recorded—the political, intellectual, and emotional tribulations of the twentieth century, it is he.

He was born in Budapest in 1905 to assimilated Jewish parents. His father was a businessman who failed most of the time but who occasionally hit the jackpot: immediately before and during the first half of World War I he made a fortune (soon lost) by manufacturing and selling soap that contained radium. Radioactivity was then a recently discovered phenomenon, and many believed the rays to be life-enhancing and disease-curing.

Koestler's father spent the rest of his days dreaming of a new product that would restore his fortune at a stroke; and, in a sense, the young Arthur shared this kind of illusion but transposed it to the intellectual, political, philosophical, and spiritual spheres. As a young man, Koestler saw in radical Zionism the answer to his existential problems, though he had no religious belief or cultural or philosophical affinities with Judaism (much later, moreover, he wrote a book still cited by anti-Zionists, *The Thirteenth Tribe*, which claims that most Jews are not of Semitic origin but descendants of the Khazars, a Turkic tribe that converted to Judaism). Then Koestler converted to orthodox Marxist communism, followed by a stage of crusading anti-communism, itself replaced by a prolonged search for a spiritualism founded on evidence and rational inference. Koestler was not a man to do things by philosophical halves: he was a drinker of infinity, to quote the title of one of his books.

Young Arthur, gifted scientifically and mathematically, studied engineering in Vienna but did not graduate. Instead the ardent Zionist went off to Palestine to live on a kibbutz. He did not last long; his personality ultimately would not allow absorption into a collective enterprise. On the verge of starvation, he was saved by a fortuitous appointment as the Palestine correspondent of the Ullstein Trust, the largest German newspaper group, which later assigned him to its Paris office. He then moved to Germany, where he served as the science editor of one newspaper and foreign editor of another, among other exploits flying in a zeppelin to the North Pole via Soviet Russia.

Koestler joined the Communist party, later explaining that it seemed the only viable alternative to Hitler, but this led Ullstein to sack him. Returning to Paris after traveling in the Soviet Union, he wrote political propaganda under Comintern direction until the outbreak of the Spanish Civil War, when a British liberal newspaper assigned him to visit Franco's headquarters. Denounced as a Communist, he managed to escape, but Franco's forces captured him during a subsequent trip to Spain and sentenced him to death. An international campaign secured his release. Koestler's years as a Comintern agent—in which he, the most egotistical of men, willingly subjected himself to the party's discipline on the grounds that it represented the sole judge of transcendent truth—gave him unparalleled insight into the psychology of party members suddenly accused of counter-revolutionary treason.

He then lived in France, breaking for good with the Communist party over the show trials. When war broke out in 1939, the French government arrested him in Paris for being a potentially hostile alien and imprisoned him in a concentration camp; a second international campaign won his freedom. Fearing re-arrest, he joined the French Foreign Legion and managed, by a very circuitous route, to reach Lisbon. From there he flew—illegally—to London, where he again found himself imprisoned, this time for six weeks. In his prison cell he corrected the proofs of *Darkness at Noon*, which would be his most famous book.

Released from prison, he at once joined the British army, which, he said, had a salutary effect upon his life. "I found myself transformed from a member of the grey, piteous crowd of refugees—the scum of earth—into a best-selling author," he wrote. "This is a dangerous experience for any writer, but before it could turn my head I was also transformed into Private No. 13805661 in 251 Company Pioneer Corps, which was not given to lionizing intellectuals." It says something of Koestler's life until then that he called the three years he spent in blitzed London, where he survived a close bombing, "among the most uneventful (I almost said peaceful) of my life."

By the age of thirty-seven, Koestler had traveled widely; spoke Hungarian, German, French, Russian, and English fluently, as well as some Hebrew (having invented the Hebrew crossword while in Palestine); had been imprisoned several times, including under sentence of death; had been a Zionist, a Communist, and an anti-Communist; and had written books in Hungarian, German, and English. Shortly after arriving in England, he knew and was friendly with its most prominent writers and intellectuals: George Orwell, Cyril Connolly, Dylan Thomas, Bertrand Russell, Alfred Ayer, and many others.

Koestler wrote *Darkness at Noon* in German while living in Paris, expecting at any moment to face arrest. It is the story of Rubashov, a Bolshevik intellectual modeled largely on Nikolai Bukharin, the economist and darling of the party who wound up executed after a 1938 Moscow show trial.

At the time of the book's publication in 1940, and for a long time afterward, the public confession of many old Bolsheviks to self-evidently absurd crimes that carried the death penalty—for example, that from the very beginning of their careers they had served foreign intelligence services—mystified many in the West. How had Communist officials obtained these confessions? Did the Russians have some extremely sophisticated and secret technique of interrogation, unknown in the West?

Of course some in the West, Communists and ardent fellow travelers, believed that the trials were fair and that the confessions were unforced and entirely veridical. Among the most influential was a prominent British lawyer, D. N. Pritt, who actually wrote a book testifying to the Moscow trials' fairness. As late as 1972 a fellow medical student, at the time a fierce Maoist, tried to convince me that the trials were genuine by lending me transcripts of the proceedings.

So Koestler's imaginary reconstruction of how Rubashov was persuaded to confess, to which he brought his own intimate knowledge of how people thought and acted who had made the party their whole life, was entirely new and original. Koestler's solution to the puzzle was that Rubashov, and those like him, confessed not because of any physical torture (though Rubashov is deprived of sleep, a technique that interrogators did use in obtaining confessions) but because it was logical for them to do so. All their adult lives they had believed that the end justified the means; moreover, and crucially, they had delegated to the party the exclusive right to judge both ends and means. Who were they, then, to object when the party decided that it needed to sacrifice them, irrespective of whether they were guilty of anything?

Koestler is sufficiently sophisticated a novelist not to make Rubashov wholly admirable. Indeed, the Communist has failed to intervene on behalf of his own secretary, Arlova, with whom he has had a love affair, when she is accused of preposterous crimes. He reasons that his life is worth more to the cause than hers.

Koestler has the aristocratic Rubashov interrogated by a proletarian functionary named Gletkin. The climax comes when Gletkin argues that Rubashov's private dissent from the party line must, logically and objectively, lead to civil war and possibly to the destruction of the dictatorship of the proletariat and that therefore his confession "is the last service the Party will require of you."

> "Comrade Rubashov, I hope that you have understood the task which the Party has set you."
>
> It was the first time that Gletkin called Rubashov "Comrade." Rubashov raised his head quickly. He felt a hot wave rising in him, against which he was helpless. His chin shook slightly while he was putting on his pince-nez.
>
> "I understand."

Here the pince-nez symbolize the last remnant of a more refined civilization (Chekhov wore them, for example), defeated by a cruder, more ruthless way of life. It is a subtle point that Koestler is making: Rubashov is both beneficiary and destroyer of the old civilization and is himself destroyed by the offspring of his own destructiveness.

Some on the right have unfairly criticized Koestler, claiming that *Darkness at Noon* implies that subtle argumentation, rather than crude torture, obtained the confessions at the Moscow trials. But nowhere in the book does Koestler suggest that harsher methods to obtain confessions did not play a role—quite the contrary—or that the methods used in Rubashov's case characterized every case. Rather, his novel is philosophical, plausibly pointing to the terrible logical and practical consequences of the belief that the ends justify the means, when those ends have been preordained by authority, whether of history, the great leader, or even God.

Darkness at Noon was probably the most influential anti-Communist book ever published, more important (in practice) even than *Animal Farm* or *Nineteen Eighty-Four*. Koestler's standing to write it was undisputed. It is true that it had little resonance in Britain, where it first appeared; and though it sold better in the United States, Communists had even less chance of success there than in Britain, so it again had muted influence. It was in France where the book's impact was decisive: there, after the war, a race took place between the publisher's printing presses and the capacity of the extremely powerful Communist party to buy up and destroy copies as they reached the bookshops. This censorship drive was an important reason why a French referendum on a new constitution, which would have given a preponderant government role to the strongest of the many political parties (then the Communists), went down to defeat. By trying to silence Koestler's book, the Communists revealed themselves as dictators in the making.

After the publication of *The God That Failed*—containing six essays by prominent intellectuals, including himself, who had been Communists but had become disillusioned to the point of fierce enmity toward their former ideal—and after his participation in the Congress for Cultural Freedom in Berlin in 1950, Koestler shifted his interest. The question of communism seemed settled beyond reasonable doubt, though in practice it needed still to be defeated. Henceforth his attention turned to science and its compatibility (or otherwise) with what one might call mystical or spiritual modes of thought.

He did not leave the practical world behind entirely. He became an ardent campaigner both against the death penalty and in favor of euthanasia (by no means an uncommon combination). His feeling against the death penalty, expressed with characteristic force in his book *Reflections on Hanging*, no doubt arose from his contact with its implementation in Franco's prison. It was also his prison experiences that gave him a lifelong interest in the welfare of prisoners and led him to establish the annual Koestler Prizes, awarded to British prisoners who had produced the best literary and artistic work in the previous year. This imaginative and wholly laudable initiative has led to the reverence shown for Koestler's name in British prisons, at least by the better-informed inmates.

Koestler's account of his internment in a Spanish prison, published first as the second half of *Spanish Testament* and then as the whole of *Dialogue with Death* (in my opinion, his greatest book), uncovers a layer of being far deeper than the political. His depiction of the way those condemned to death were taken away to execution is unforgettable:

> I had gone to sleep, and I woke up shortly before midnight. In the black silence of the prison, charged with the nightmares of thirteen hundred sleeping men, I heard the murmured prayer of a priest and the ringing of the sanctus bell.
>
> Then a cell door . . . was opened, and a name was softly called out. "*Qué?*"—What is the matter—asked a sleepy voice, and the priest's voice grew clearer and the bell rang louder.
>
> And now the drowsy man understood. At first he only groaned; then in a dull voice he called for help: "*Socorro, socorro.*"

The same scene is enacted at another cell:

> Again, "*Qué?*" And again the prayer and the bell. This one sobbed and whimpered like a child. Then he cried out for his mother: "*Madre, madre!*"

And again: "*Madre, madre!*"

And in his description of the last man removed for execution that night, Koestler subtly indicates the complete inadequacy of political ideology in the face of the mysteries of life and death:

> They went to the next cell. . . . He asked no questions. While the priest prayed, he began in a low voice to sing the "Marseillaise." But after a few bars his voice broke, and he too sobbed. They marched him off.
>
> And then there was silence again.

No revolutionary triumphalism here, with heroes gladly going to their death in the knowledge that the cause will ultimately triumph.

Throughout *Dialogue with Death*, Koestler raises profound existential questions. He becomes almost mystical, foreshadowing his later interests; after his release, he dreams of the Seville prison. "Often when I wake at night I am homesick for my cell in the death-house . . . and I feel I have never been so free as I was then." He continues:

> This is a very curious feeling indeed. We lived an unusual life. . . . The constant nearness of death weighed us down and at the same time gave us a feeling of weightless floating. We were without responsibility. Most of us were not afraid of death, only of the act of dying; and there were times when we overcame even this fear. At such moments we were free—men without shadows, dismissed from the ranks of the mortal; it was the most complete experience of freedom that can be granted a man.

The man who wrote those words was not likely to remain a Communist (as he was when he wrote them). Indeed, it is clear that his initial attraction to communism must have been religious—not that he saw it as the best doctrine with which to oppose Hitler, as he claimed in his subsequent self-justification, or that it represented for him a supposedly pure, rational philosophy. When Koestler saw what communism wrought, both materially and in men's souls, he realized that it could never answer his religious needs.

While he had those needs, he was sufficiently a man of the Enlightenment not to be able to subscribe to any traditional religion. In the 1960s, after all, he produced massive histories of science that commanded the respect of prominent scientists; yet he could not believe that science, at least as then practiced, contained all the answers he sought. In his novel *The Age of Longing*, Koestler describes the plight of Hydie, a lapsed Catholic:

> Oh, if only she could go back to the infinite comfort of father confessors and mother superiors, of a well-ordered hierarchy which promised punishment and reward, and furnished the world with justice and meaning. If only she could go back! But she was under the curse of reason, which rejected whatever might quench her thirst, without abolishing the urge; which rejected the answer without abolishing the question. For the place of God had become vacant, and there was a draught blowing through the world as in an empty flat before the new tenants have arrived.

Precisely Koestler's own predicament, and that of modern man. It is no wonder that, a few years later, he went to India and Japan to seek the mystical wisdom of Hinduism and Zen Buddhism, or that he sought evidence of man's nonmateriality in experiments to prove the reality of extrasensory perception, only a short step from full-blown spiritualism.

Koestler was fully aware, from an early age, of the contradictions in his own character, which helps make him one of the great autobiographers of the last century. In *Arrow in the Blue*, the first volume of his autobiography, he sums himself up as an adolescent: "The youth of sixteen that I was, with the plastered-down hair, and the fatuous smirk, at once arrogant and sheepish, was emotionally seasick: greedy for pleasure, haunted by guilt, torn between feelings of inferiority and superiority, between the need for contemplative solitude and the frustrated urge for gregariousness."

And at the end of *The Invisible Writing*, the second volume, Koestler says: "The contradictions between sensitivity and callousness, integrity and shadiness, egomania and self-sacrifice which appear in every chapter [of the autobiography] would never add up to a credible character in a novel; but this is not a novel. . . . The seemingly paradoxical can be resolved only by holding the figure against the background of his time, by taking into account both the historian's and the psychologist's approach."

It is precisely because Koestler's life and work so deeply instantiate the existential dilemmas of our age that he is a fascinating figure, unjustly neglected, and too often dismissed as a sexual psychopath. He was not a naturally good man (far from it), but he was struggling toward the good by the light and authority of his own intellect; unfortunately, as Hume tells us, reason is the slave of the passions, and Koestler was an exceptionally passionate man.

Once I happened to find two first editions, very cheap, of Koestler's books in a secondhand bookshop that I haunt. "Ah," said the bookshop owner, "*The Age of Longing* and *Dialogue with Death*: a complete summary of human life, when you come to think of it."

2007

Ibsen and His Discontents

◆ A FAMILY, Dr. Johnson once wrote, is a little kingdom, torn with factions and exposed to revolutions. This is a less than ringing endorsement of family life, of course; and the great Norwegian playwright Henrik Ibsen, whose childhood had been as unhappy as Johnson's, would have agreed with this assessment. But Johnson, unlike Ibsen, went on to remark that all judgment is comparative: that to judge an institution or a convention rightly, one must compare it with its alternatives. Marriage has many pains, says Johnson in *Rasselas*, but celibacy has no pleasures.

Johnson saw human existence as inseparable from dissatisfaction. It is man's nature to suffer from incompatible desires simultaneously—for example, wanting both security and excitement. When he has one, he longs for the other, so that contentment is rarely unalloyed and never lasting.

But most people find it more comforting to believe in perfectibility than in imperfectibility—an example of what Dr. Johnson called the triumph of hope over experience. The notion of imperfectibility not only fans existential anxieties but also—by precluding simple solutions to all human problems—places much tougher intellectual demands upon us than utopianism does. Not every question can be answered by reference to a few simple abstract principles that, if followed with sufficient rigor, will supposedly lead to perfection—which is why conservatism is so much more difficult to reduce to slogans than its much more abstract competitors.

The yearning for principles that will abolish human dissatisfactions helps account for the continuing popularity of Ibsen's three most frequently performed plays: *A Doll's House*, *Ghosts*, and *Hedda Gabler*. Each is a ferocious attack on marriage as a powerful source of much human unhappiness and frustration. It is this indictment that gives Ibsen his extraordinary modernity, a modernity that has only seemed to increase over the century and a quarter since he wrote these plays.

The scale of Ibsen's achievement is astonishing. Almost single-handedly he gave birth to the modern theater. Before him the nineteenth century, so rich in other literary forms, produced hardly a handful of plays that can still be performed, and the literary power of his work has never since been equaled. It was he who first realized that mundane daily life, relayed in completely naturalistic language, contained within it all the ingredients of tragedy. That he should have transformed the whole of Western drama while writing in an obscure language that was considered primitive—and that he should have produced in twenty years more performable plays than all the British and French playwrights of his era put together, despite their incomparably longer and richer theatrical traditions—is almost miraculous.

Though Ibsen often claimed to be a poet rather than a social critic, lacking any didactic purpose, the evidence of his letters and speeches (quite apart from the internal evidence of the plays themselves) proves quite the opposite—that he was almost incandescent with moral purpose. Contemporaries had no doubt of it; and the first book about him in English, Bernard Shaw's *Quintessence of Ibsenism*, published in 1891 while Ibsen still had many years to live and plays to write, stated forthrightly that his works stood or fell by the moral precepts they advocated. Shaw thought that Ibsen was a Joshua come to blow down the walls of moral convention. I think this judgment is wrong: Ibsen was far too great a writer to be only a moralist, and it is possible still to read or watch his plays with pleasure and instruction without swallowing what he has to say hook, line, and sinker.

Still, Ibsen's influence extended far beyond the theater. He wrote as much to be read as to be performed; and his plays were published, often in relatively large editions, to catch the Christmas market. And Shaw was hardly alone in perceiving their unconventionality. *Ghosts*, for instance, was initially considered so controversial, not to say filthy, that its printed version was handed round semi-clandestinely, few people daring to be seen reading it. By the end of his life, however, a quarter of a century later, most European intellectuals had come to take its moral outlook virtually for granted, and anyone who continued to resist its teachings seemed mired in an unenlightened past.

The comparatively easy acceptance of what Shaw called Ibsenism—twenty or thirty years is a long time in the life of a man, but not of mankind—means that Ibsen must have expressed what many people had thought and wanted to hear but had not dared to say. He was thus both a cause and a symptom of social change; and like many such figures, he was partly right and largely wrong.

What are his moral teachings, at least in the three plays that have forged his enduring image? He was as rabidly hostile to conventional family life as Marx or Engels, but he was a much more effective and powerful critic, because his criticism did not remain on the level of philosophical abstraction. On the contrary, he laid bare the factions and revolutions of family life, its lies and miseries, in compelling and believable dramas; and while it has always been open to the reader or viewer to ascribe the moral pathology exhibited in these plays to the particular characters or neuroses of their dramatis personae alone, clearly this was not Ibsen's intention. He was not a forerunner of Jerry Springer; his aim was not titillation or a mere display of the grotesque. He intends us to regard the morbidity his plays anatomize as typical and quintessential (to use Shaw's word), the inevitable consequence of certain social conventions and institutions. He invites us implicitly, and explicitly in *A Doll's House* and *Ghosts*, to consider alternative ways of living in order to eliminate what he considers the avoidable misery of the pathology he brings to light.

It is hardly surprising that feminists celebrate Ibsen. For one thing, his three oft-performed plays repeatedly suggest that marriage is but formalized and legalized prostitution. In *A Doll's House*, Mrs. Linde, a childhood friend whom Nora has just encountered after an absence of many years, tells Nora that her marriage has been an unhappy one (I use throughout Michael Meyer's excellent translations):

> NORA: Tell me, is it really true that you didn't love your husband? . . .
>
> MRS. LINDE: Well, my mother was still alive; and she was helpless and bedridden. And I had my two little brothers to take care of. I didn't feel I could say no.
>
> NORA: . . . He was rich then, was he?

In *Ghosts*, too, marriage for money is a prominent theme. The carpenter Engstrand suggests to Regina, who at this point thinks she is his daughter, that she should marry for that reason. After all, he himself married Regina's mother for money. Like Regina, she had been a servant in the Alving household, until Lieutenant Alving got her pregnant. Mrs. Alving discharged her, giving her some money before she left, and then Engstrand married her. Pastor Manders discusses the matter with Lieutenant Alving's widow:

> MANDERS: How much was it you gave the girl?
>
> MRS. ALVING: Fifty pounds.
>
> MANDERS: Just imagine! To go and marry a fallen woman for a paltry fifty pounds!

The implication is that the transaction would have been reasonable, in the eyes of the respectable pastor, if the sum had been larger—as large as the sum that had "bought" Mrs. Alving. At the play's outset, when she is making arrangements for the opening of an orphanage named in memory of her husband, she explains something to Pastor Manders:

MRS. ALVING: The annual donations that I have made to this Orphanage add up to the sum . . . which made Lieutenant Alving, in his day, "a good match."
MANDERS: I understand—
MRS. ALVING: It was the sum with which he bought me.

Hedda Gabler alludes only slightly less directly to the mercenary motive of marriage. Mrs. Elvsted is another old acquaintance of the main female character, who turns up after an absence of many years and has had an unhappy marriage. She went to Mr. Elvsted as a housekeeper and, after the death of his first wife, married him:

HEDDA: But he loves you, surely? In his own way?
MRS. ELVSTED: Oh, I don't know. I think he finds me useful. And then I don't cost much to keep. I'm cheap.

Marriage, then, is a financial bargain, and a pretty poor one—at least for women. But, of course, there are other reasons for marital unhappiness, especially the irreducible incompatibility of husband and wife. In fact any apparent happiness is a façade or a lie, maintained by social pressure.

In *A Doll's House*, for example, Nora appears at first to be happily married to Torvald Helmer, a young lawyer on his way up. Helmer treats her like a little girl, sometimes chiding and sometimes indulging her, but never taking her seriously as an adult; and she plays along, acting the featherbrained young woman to almost nauseating perfection. Unbeknownst to Helmer, however, Nora has previously saved his life by obtaining a loan, secured by a forged signature, that allowed them to spend a year in Italy, whose warmer climate cured the disease that would have killed him.

When Helmer discovers what she has done, he is not grateful and does not see her forgery as a manifestation of her love for him; on the contrary, he condemns her unmercifully and tells her that she is not fit to be mother to their three children. Helmer interprets the episode as if he were the lawyer prosecuting her rather than her husband.

The scales fall from Nora's eyes. Their life together, she sees, has been not only an outward but an inward sham: he is not the man that she, blinded by her acceptance of the social role assigned to her, took him for. She tells him that she is leaving him; and although Helmer offers a more adult, equal relationship between them, it is too late.

Undoubtedly Ibsen was pointing to a genuine and serious problem of the time—the assumed inability of women to lead any but a domestic existence, without intellectual content (and, in fact, the play was based upon a real case). But if this were its principal moral focus, the play would have lost its impact by now, since the point has long been conceded. Ibsen was not, in fact, a devotee of women's rights: addressing a conference on the subject in Oslo, he said, "I have never written any play to further a social purpose. . . . I am not even very sure what Women's Rights really are." With no faith in legislative or institutional solutions to problems, Ibsen had a much larger target: the change of people from within, so that they might finally express their true nature unmediated by the distortions of society.

In *Ghosts*, Mrs. Alving's marriage is unhappy not just because she was "bought." Her husband was a philandering alcoholic, and she fled from him after a year of marriage, taking refuge in Pastor Manders's house. Although Manders and Mrs. Alving felt a mutual attraction—indeed, fell in love—the pastor persuaded her that she had a religious duty to return to her husband. Despite Alving's promise to change, which at the beginning of the play Pastor Manders believes that he kept, Alving continued his dissolute ways until his death. Mrs. Alving made it her task to conceal his conduct from the world and from her son, Oswald. But when Alving impregnated the servant with Regina (who is thus Oswald's half-sister), she sent Oswald away and would not allow him to return home while Alving was still alive. While Alving drank himself to death, Mrs. Alving made a success of his estate—a success that she allowed to be attributed to Alving, permitting him to die in the odor not only of sanctity but of success.

The lies of Mrs. Alving's life spring from the false sense of shame—what will others say?—that traps her into returning to Alving and into covering up for him. Similarly, Manders, as Ibsen portrays him, represents a bogus moralism, in whose code appearance is more important than reality or inner meaning, and avoidance of shame is a better guide to conduct than conscience. This code leads Manders to make wrong decisions even in banal practical matters—for example, whether the orphanage should be insured or not. He discusses this question with Mrs. Alving, noting that there had nearly been a fire there the day before. Mrs. Alving concludes that the orphanage should be insured. But then Manders indulges in a little oily and dishonest sanctimony:

MANDERS: Ah, but wait a minute, Mrs. Alving. Let us consider this question a little more closely. . . . The Orphanage is, so to speak, to be consecrated to a higher purpose. . . . As far as I personally am concerned, I see nothing offensive in securing ourselves against all eventualities. . . . But what is the feeling among the local people out here? . . . Are there many people with the right to an opinion . . . who might take offense? . . . I am thinking chiefly of people sufficiently independent and influential to make it impossible for one to ignore their opinions altogether. . . . You see! In town we have

a great many such people. Followers of other denomina-
tions. People might very easily come to the conclusion that
neither you nor I have sufficient trust in the ordinance of a
Higher Power. . . . I know—my conscience is clear, that is
true. But all the same, we couldn't prevent a false and un-
favorable interpretation being placed on our action. . . .
And I can't altogether close my eyes to the difficult—I might
even say deeply embarrassing—position in which I might
find myself.

Of course the opinions of the people whom Manders is pro-
pitiating are just as bogus as his own; and when, the next day,
the orphanage does in fact burn down, because of Manders's
carelessness with a candle, he not only deems it God's judgment
on the Alving family but is clearly worried more about his own
reputation than about anything else. In fact he finds someone
else—Engstrand, the carpenter—willing to take the blame for
what he has done. Manders has no conscience, only a fear of
what others will say.

His explanation of why he persuaded Mrs. Alving to return
to her husband displays the same pharisaical fear of public
opinion:

> MANDERS: . . . a wife is not appointed to be her husband's judge.
> It was your duty humbly to bear that cross which a higher
> will had seen fit to assign to you. But instead you . . . haz-
> ard your good name, and very nearly ruin the reputation of
> others.
>
> MRS. ALVING: Others? Another's, you mean?
>
> MANDERS: It was extremely inconsiderate of you to seek refuge
> with me.

Once again there can be no doubt that Ibsen has most accurately put his finger on a pseudo-morality in which shame or
social disapproval takes the place of personal conscience or
true moral principle, and in whose name people—especially

women—are made to suffer misery, degradation, and even violence. This is no mere figment of Ibsen's imagination. Indeed, I have observed the consequences of the operation of this pseudo-morality among my young Muslim patients, who are made to suffer the torments of a living hell and are sometimes even killed by their male relatives, solely to preserve the "good name" of the family in the opinion of others.

By no means, then, was Ibsen exaggerating. When he said that his fellow countrymen were a nation of serfs living in a free country, he meant that their fear of shame and notions of respectability enslaved and oppressed them, even in a land without political oppression.

The third of these portraits of unhappy marriages, *Hedda Gabler*, is the least interesting because it is implausible. Hedda Gabler, the daughter of a general, marries beneath herself, choosing an intellectual who hopes for a chair at the university, though he is actually a petty pedant, without originality or flair. In fact he is such a milksop, such a pathetic ninny, that it is hard to believe that Hedda, with her very high conception of her own abilities and entitlements, would have married him in the first place. It is therefore difficult to take her consequent travails very seriously. But she ends up killing herself because life, with the bourgeois options it currently offers her, is not worth living.

It is in *A Doll's House* and *Ghosts* that Ibsen offers us not just criticisms but positive prescriptions. And it is because his prescriptions are those of the 1960s, though written eighty years earlier, that we find him still so astonishingly modern and prescient.

When, in *A Doll's House*, Nora tells her husband that she is leaving him, he asks her (just as Pastor Manders would have done) whether she has thought of what other people will say. He then goes on to ask her about her duty:

HELMER : Can you neglect your most sacred duties?
NORA: What do you call my most sacred duties?

HELMER: Do I have to tell you? Your duties to your husband, and your children.

This crucial passage continues with a little psychobabble followed by the justification of radical egotism:

NORA: I have another duty which is equally sacred.
HELMER: . . . What on earth could that be?
NORA: My duty to myself.

Nora goes on to explain that she is first and foremost a human being—or that, anyway, she must try to become one. (This sentiment reminds one of Marx's view that men will become truly human only after the revolution has brought about the end of class society. All who had gone before, apparently—and all of Marx's contemporaries—were less than truly human. Little wonder that untold millions were done to death by those who shared this philosophy.) So if Nora is not yet a human being, what will make her one? Philosophical autonomy is the answer:

NORA: . . . I'm no longer prepared to accept what people say and what's written in books. I must think things out for myself and try to find my own answer.

And the criterion she is to use, to judge whether her own answer is correct, is whether it is right—"or anyway, whether it is right for me." Postmodernism is not so very modern after all, it seems: Ibsen got there first.

Moments later, Nora makes clear what the consequences of her new freedom are:

NORA: I don't want to see the children. . . . As I am now I can be nothing to them.

And with these chilling words she severs all connection with her three children, forever. Her duty to herself leaves no room for a moment's thought for them. They are as dust in the balance.

When, as I have, you have met hundreds, perhaps thousands, of people abandoned in their childhood by one or both of their parents, on essentially the same grounds ("I need my own space"), and you have seen the lasting despair and damage that such abandonment causes, you cannot read or see *A Doll's House* without anger and revulsion. Now we see what Ibsen meant when he said that women's rights were of no fundamental interest to him. He was out to promote something much more important: universal egotism.

It is clear from *Ghosts* as well that Ibsen conceived of a society in which everyone was his own Descartes, working out everything from first principles—or at least what he or she believed to be first principles. For example, when Pastor Manders arrives for the first time in Mrs. Alving's house, he finds some books that he considers dangerously liberal:

MRS. ALVING: But what do you object to in these books?

MANDERS : Object to? You surely don't imagine I spend my time studying such publications?

MRS. ALVING: In other words, you've no idea what you're condemning?

MANDERS : I've read quite enough about these writings to disapprove of them.

MRS. ALVING: Don't you think you ought to form your own opinion—?

MANDERS: My dear Mrs. Alving, there are many occasions in life when one must rely on the judgment of others.

Coming from a character whom Ibsen scorns as ridiculous and bigoted, these words, which contain an obvious truth, are meant to be rejected out of hand. In Ibsen's philosophy, everyone—at least Nature's aristocrats, for in fact Ibsen was no egalitarian or democrat—must examine every question for himself and arrive at his own answer: for example, whether the *Protocols of the Elders of Zion* is historically true—or at least historically true for him.

The object, or at least the obvious consequence, of such independence of judgment is the breakdown of the artificial, socially constructed barriers that constrain behavior and (in theory) prevent people from reaching a state of complete
happiness, which is to say absence of frustration. Unhappiness
in all the plays results from not having followed the heart's inclinations, either by not doing what one wants, or by doing
what one does not want, all to comply with some social obligation enforced by the Pastor Manderses of the world:

> MANDERS: . . . your marriage was celebrated in an orderly fash-
> ion and in full accordance with the law.
> MRS. ALVING: All this talk about law and order. I often think that
> is what causes all the unhappiness in the world.

Mrs. Alving's son, Oswald, has returned home from Paris
not only to attend the opening of the orphanage named for his
father but also because he is ill, with tertiary syphilis. He is destined to die soon in a state of either madness or dementia, according to the Parisian specialist (French syphilologists knew
more about the disease than any other doctors in the world, and
Ibsen was always well informed about medical matters).

At first Oswald—still believing that his father was a fine, up-
standing man—concludes that he contracted the disease by his
own conduct. In fact he has congenital syphilis, passed on by his
father. (It was formerly objected that Oswald could not have
caught syphilis from his father alone, but in fact Oswald's father
could have passed on the germs to Oswald through his mother,
infecting her only with a subclinical case.) For her part, Mrs.
Alving is in no doubt that society is responsible for her husband's (and thus her son's) disease:

> MRS. ALVING: And this happy, carefree child—for he [Alving]
> was like a child, then—had to live here in a little town that
> had no joy to offer him. . . . And in the end the inevitable
> happened. . . . Your poor father never found any outlet for

the joy of life that was in him. And I didn't bring any sunshine into his home. . . . They had taught me about duty and things like that and I sat here for too long believing in them. In the end everything became a matter of duty—my duty, and his duty, and—I'm afraid I made his home intolerable for your poor father.

The way of avoiding such tragedies is for everyone to follow his own inclinations, more or less as they arise.

Only associations free of institutional constraint will set men free. Earlier in the play Oswald has described to the scandalized Manders the informal families among whom he mixed in bohemian Paris, after Manders tells Mrs. Alving that Oswald has never had the opportunity to know a real home.

OSWALD : I beg your pardon, sir, but there you're quite mistaken.

MANDERS: Oh? I thought you had spent practically all your time in artistic circles.

OSWALD : I have.

MANDERS : Mostly among young artists.

OSWALD : Yes.

MANDERS : But I thought most of those people lacked the means to support a family and make a home for themselves.

OSWALD : Some of them can't afford to get married, sir.

MANDERS : Yes, that's what I'm saying.

OSWALD : But that doesn't mean they can't have a home. . . .

MANDERS : But I'm not speaking about bachelor establishments. By a home I mean a family establishment, where a man lives with his wife and children.

OSWALD: Quite. Or with his children and their mother.

We go on to learn that these informal families, precisely because they are based not upon convention, duty, or social pressure but upon unconstrained love, are not only equal to conventional families but much superior. Oswald talks of the peace and harmony that he found among them: "I have never heard an offensive word there, far less ever witnessed anything that could be called immoral."

And he adds:

OSWALD : No; do you know when and where I have encountered immorality in artistic circles?

MANDERS : No, I don't, thank heaven.

OSWALD: Well, I shall tell you. I have encountered it when one or another of our model husbands and fathers came down to look around a little on their own. . . . Then we learned a few things. Those gentlemen were able to tell us about places and things of which we had never dreamed.

Not only are informal arrangements happier, therefore, than formal ones, but they prevent the spread of the very syphilis from which Oswald suffers. Suffice it to say that this has not been my experience of the last fifteen years of medical practice.

The right—indeed, the duty—of everyone to decide his own moral principles and to decide what is right for him, without the ghosts of the past to misguide him, leads Mrs. Alving to approve of incest, if incest is what makes people happy. While Oswald is still unaware that Regina is his half-sister, he falls in love with her (very quickly, it must be said), and she with him. He wants to marry her.

Mrs. Alving discusses the matter with Manders, who by now is aware of the consanguinity of Oswald and Regina:

MANDERS: . . . That would be dreadful.

MRS. ALVING: If I knew . . . that it would make him happy—

MANDERS: Yes? What then?

MRS. ALVING: If only I weren't such an abject coward, I'd say to him: "Marry her, or make what arrangements you please. As long as you're honest and open about it—"

MANDERS: . . . You mean a legal marriage! . . . It's absolutely unheard of—!

MRS. ALVING: Unheard of, did you say? Put your hand on your heart, Pastor Manders, and tell me—do you really believe there aren't married couples like that to be found in this country?

This is an argument typical of people who wish to abolish boundaries: if these boundaries are not—because they cannot be—adhered to with perfect consistency, then they should be obliterated, as they can only give rise to hypocrisy. Mrs. Alving adds the kind of smart-aleck comment that has ever been the stock-in-trade of those to whom boundaries are so irksome: "Well, we all stem from a relationship of that kind, so we are told."

It is not that Mrs. Alving fails to believe in right and wrong. But what is wrong is betrayal of one's inclinations. When Manders describes his painful self-control in sending her back to her husband when he was in love with her himself, he asks whether that was a crime. Mrs. Alving replies, "Yes, I think so."

By the end of the play Oswald has asked his mother to kill him with a morphine injection if he has another attack of madness or dementia. In the last scene Oswald does have such an attack, and Mrs. Alving's last words in the play, concerning this act of euthanasia, are, "No; no; no! Yes! No; no!" We never find out whether she goes ahead, and Ibsen refused to say. But he clearly saw it as a matter for everyone to make up his own mind about, to work out for himself, free of legal—which is to say, conventional and institutional—guidance.

The modernity of Ibsen's thought hardly needs further emphasis. The elevation of emotion over principle, of inclination over duty, of rights over responsibilities, of ego over the claims of others; the impatience with boundaries and the promotion of the self as the measure of all things: what could be more modern or gratifying to our current sensibility? Not surprisingly, Ibsen regarded youth rather than age as the fount of wisdom.

"Youth," he assures us, "has an instinctive genius which unconsciously hits upon the right answer."

And Ibsen was profoundly modern in another respect, too. In his own existence he was very conventional. Although attracted to women other than his wife, he always resisted temptation; he dressed correctly; he ostentatiously wore the decorations awarded him by the crowned heads of Europe—which, notoriously, he solicited. He was extremely cautious and careful with money. His habits and tastes were profoundly bourgeois, and he was regular in his habits to the point of rigidity. He could be extremely prickly when he felt his own dignity affronted, and he was a great lover of formality. His wife called him Ibsen, and he signed his letters to her Henrik Ibsen, not Henrik.

His character was formed in an atmosphere of Protestant Pietism. He was inhibited to a degree unusual even among his compatriots. As a child he experienced the trauma of his father's bankruptcy and the descent from prosperity and social respect to poverty and humiliation. He both hated the society in which he grew up and craved high status within it.

Ibsen's character was fixed, but he longed to be different. He was Calvin wanting to be Dionysius. If he couldn't change himself, at least he could change others, and society itself. Like many modern intellectuals, he had difficulty distinguishing his personal problems and neuroses from social problems. Shortly before he wrote *Ghosts*, his son, Sigurd, who had lived almost all his life abroad, had been refused admission to Christiania (Oslo) University by the governing ecclesiastical authorities until he had met such entry requirements as a test of proficiency in Norwegian. Ibsen was furious. He wrote, "I shall raise a memorial to that black band of theologians." And he did—Pastor Manders.

There is no evidence that Ibsen ever thought, much less cared, about the effect of his principles on society as a whole. This indifference is hardly surprising, given that he thought that nothing good could come of the great herd of mankind, which he termed the majority, the masses, the mob. He believed that he himself belonged to an aristocracy of intellect, and it is of course in the nature of aristocrats that they should have privileges not accorded to others. But whether we like it or not, we live in a democratic age, when the privileges claimed by some will soon be claimed by all. The charmingly insouciant free love of bohemians is soon enough transmuted into the violent chaos of the slums.

"[*Ghosts*] contains the future," said Ibsen. He also said that he is most right who is most in tune with the future. But he did not display any interest or foresight into what that future might contain: for him, not whatever is, is right, but whatever will be, is right. Whether the scores of millions who suffered and died in the twentieth century because of the destruction of moral boundaries would have agreed with him is another matter.

2005

The Specters
Haunting Dresden

THE FOUNDATIONS of Hitler's bunker were uncovered during the building frenzy in Berlin that followed the reunification of Germany. An anguished debate ensued about what to do with the site, for in Germany both memory and amnesia are dangerous, each with its moral hazards. To mark the bunker's site might turn it into a place of pilgrimage for neo-Nazis, resurgent in the East; not to mark it might be regarded as an attempt to deny the past. In the end, anonymous burial was deemed the better, which is to say the safer, option.

Nowhere in the world (except, perhaps, in Israel or Russia) does history weigh as heavily, as palpably, upon ordinary people as in Germany. Sixty years after the end of World War II, the disaster of Nazism is still unmistakably and inescapably inscribed upon almost every town and cityscape, in whichever direction you look. The urban environment of Germany, whose towns and cities were once among the most beautiful in the world, second only to Italy's, is now a wasteland of functional yet discordant modern architecture, soulless and incapable of inspiring anything but a vague existential unease, with a sense of impermanence and unreality that mere prosperity can do nothing to dispel. Well-stocked shops do not supply meaning or purpose. Beauty, at least in its man-made form, has left the land for good; and such remnants of past glories as remain serve only as a constant, nagging reminder of what has been lost, destroyed, utterly and irretrievably smashed up.

Nor are the comforts of victimhood available to the Germans as they survey the devastation of their homeland. Walking with the widow of a banker through the one small square in Frankfurt that has been restored to its medieval splendor, I remarked how beautiful a city Frankfurt must once have been, and how terrible it was that such beauty should have been lost forever.

"We started it," she said. "We got what we deserved."

But who was this "we" of whom she spoke? She was not of an age to have helped or even to have supported the Nazis, and therefore (if justice requires that each should get his desert) it was unjust that she should bear the guilty burden of the past. And Germans far younger than she still bear it. I went to dinner with a young businessman, born twenty years after the end of the war, who told me that the forestry company for which he worked, and which had interests in Britain, had decided that it needed a mission statement. A meeting ensued, and someone suggested *Holz mit Stolz* ("Wood with Pride"), whereupon a two-hour discussion erupted among the employees of the company as to whether pride in anything was permitted to the Germans, or whether it was the beginning of the slippery slope that led to . . . well, everyone knew where. The businessman found this all perfectly normal, part of being a contemporary German.

Collective pride is denied the Germans because, if pride is taken in the achievements of one's national ancestors, it follows that shame for what they have done must also be accepted. And the shame of German history is greater than any cultural achievement, not because that achievement fails to balance the shame but because it is more recent than any achievement, and furthermore was committed by a generation either still living or still existent well within living memory.

The moral impossibility of patriotism worries Germans of conservative instinct or temperament. Upon what in their historical tradition can they safely look back as a guide or a help? One young German conservative historian I met took refuge in Anglophilia—his England, of course, being an England of the past. He needed a refuge, because Hitler and Nazism had besmirched everything in his own land. The historiography that sees in German history nothing but a prelude to Hitler and Nazism may be intellectually unjustified, the product of the historian's bogus authorial omniscience, but it has emotional and psychological force nonetheless, precisely because the willingness to take pride in the past implies a preparedness to accept the shame of it. Thus Bach and Beethoven can be celebrated, but not as Germans; otherwise they would be tainted. The young German historian worked for a publishing house with a history lasting almost four centuries, but its failure to go out of business during the twelve years of the Third Reich cast a shadow both forward and backward, like a spectral presence that haunts a great mansion.

The impossibility of patriotism does not extinguish the need to belong, however. No man is, or can be, an island; everyone, no matter how egotistical, needs to belong to a collectivity larger than himself. A young German once said to me, "I don't feel German, I feel European." This sounded false to my ears: it had the same effect upon me as the squeal of chalk on a blackboard, and sent a shiver down my spine. One might as well say, "I don't feel human, I feel mammalian." We do not, and cannot, feel all that we are: so that while we who live in Europe are European, we don't feel European.

In any case, can a German feel European unilaterally, without the Portuguese (for example) similarly and reciprocally feeling European rather than Portuguese? From my observations of the French, they still feel French, indeed quite strongly so. Nearly half a century after the Treaty of Rome, they can't be said to like the Germans; to think otherwise is to mistake a marriage of convenience for the passion of Romeo and Juliet.

A common European identity therefore has to be forged deliberately and artificially; and one of the imperatives for attempting to do so is the need of Germans for an identity that is not German (the other, which dovetails neatly, is the French drive to recover world power). And since the Germans are very powerful in Europe, by weight of their economy, their need to escape from themselves by absorbing everyone into a new collective identity will sooner or later be perceived in the rest of Europe as the need to impose themselves—as a return to their bad old habits. New identities can indeed be forged, but usually in the crucible of war or at least of social upheaval: not, in the context, an inviting prospect.

On no city does history weigh heavier than on Dresden. It is sixty-three years since the bombing that forever changed the basis of the city's renown. Overnight, the Florence of the Elbe became a perpetual monument to destruction from the air, famed for its rubble and its corpses rather than its baroque architecture and its devotion to art. And then came communism.

You meet people in Dresden who, until a few years ago, knew nothing but life under Hitler, Ulbricht, and Honecker. Truly the sins of their fathers were visited upon them, for they brought neither the Nazis nor the Communists to power, and there was nothing they could do to escape them. For such people the sudden change in 1990 was both liberation and burden. Avid to see a world that had been previously forbidden them, they took immediate advantage of their new freedom to visit the farthest areas of the globe, the more exotic the better. But the liberation brought with it a heightened awareness of the man-made desert of their own pasts, seven-eighths of their lives, truly an expense of spirit in a waste of shame. Never was Joy's grape burst more decisively against veil'd Melancholy's palate fine.

A decade and a half, and untold billions of deutsche marks and euros later, Dresden is still incompletely Westernized. Its unemployment rate is three times that of Germany as a whole, so high in fact that all the city dwellers I met believed the official figures to be manipulated downward, for propaganda purposes: it being inconceivable to them, as the result of long and incontrovertible experience, that any government would tell the truth about anything. And while some parts of the city have taken on the feverish vulgarity that for so many people in the modern world is the manifestation, prerequisite, and only meaning and value of freedom, others still have that disintegrating deadness peculiar to communism, where paint flakes and stucco crumbles, where stale smells always linger in stairwells and electric light casts a yellowing gloom the color of cheap paper that has aged.

Not all Dresden was bombed, of course; on the banks of the Elbe there are still the magnificent villas of the haute bourgeoisie. Some of them have been bought and restored by rich "Wessis," as the inhabitants of the former West Germany are still, not altogether affectionately, known; but others remain unrestored, uninhabited, and deteriorating, at night appearing unlit, like the set of a Gothic horror movie. One expects bats or vampires to emerge. For more than forty years they were the homes of Dresden "workers of the brain" (to use Communist terminology), but such was their dilapidation that, immediately after reunification, they were declared unfit for habitation according to the standards of the West, and their residents moved elsewhere.

To the moral complications of a Nazi past were added those of a Communist past, the greatest of which was an awareness of just how widespread the practice of denunciation had been. On some estimates a sixth of the population of the former German Democratic Republic were *Mitarbeiter*—collaborators with the secret police, the Stasi—and had spied upon and denounced their neighbors, friends, relatives, and even spouses. Once the archives opened and people could read their security dossiers for themselves, they discovered in many cases that those to whom they had relayed their private thoughts had relayed them in turn to the Stasi, in return, practically, for nothing except the informer's satisfaction of being on the right side of the powerful. Those whom people had thought were their best friends turned out to be the very ones whose denunciation had resulted in their otherwise inexplicable failure to gain promotion in their work, sometimes for decades. Such discoveries were not conducive to a favorable or an optimistic view of human nature or the trust upon which a secure social life is built. The GDR, founded on a political theory that made a fetish of human solidarity, turned everyone into an atom in the asocial ether.

The destruction of Dresden on the night of February 13, 1945, by the Royal Air Force, and on the following two days by the U.S. Army Air Corps, necessitated the rebuilding of the city, with only a small area around the famous Zwinger restored to its former glory. Dresden had been all but destroyed once before, by the armies of Frederick the Great (if Frederick was enlightened, give me obscurantism); but at least he replaced the Renaissance city recorded in the canvases of Bellotto with a baroque one, not with a wilderness of totalitarian functionalism whose purpose was to stamp out all sense of individuality and to emphasize the omnipresent might of the state. The bombing of Dresden was a convenient pretext to do what Communists (and some others) like to do in any case: the systematization of Bucharest during Ceauşescu's rule, or the replacement of the medieval city of Alès, twenty-five miles from my house in France, by mass housing of hideous inhumanity on the orders of the Communist city council, being but two cases in point.

Despite this, the Communists used the destruction of Dresden for propaganda purposes throughout the four decades of their rule. The church bells of the city tolled on every anniversary of the bombing, for the twenty minutes it took the RAF to unload the explosives that created the firestorm that turned the Florence of the Elbe into a smoking ruin as archaeological as Pompeii. "See what the capitalist barbarians did," was the message, "and what they would do again if they had the chance and if we did not arm ourselves to the teeth." Needless to say, the rapine of the Red Army went strictly unmentioned.

But the bombing caused some unease in Britain even at the time. Was it justified? The issue of the war, after all, was by then hardly in doubt; and, in any case, both the ethics and efficacy of bombing civilian areas had been questioned, not only by left-wing politicians and George Bell, bishop of Chichester, but by the air force commanders themselves. A debate has simmered ever since, occasionally coming to a boil, as when a statue commemorating the head of the RAF's Bomber Command, Arthur Harris, was unveiled in London in 1992 or, more recently, when the queen paid a state visit to Germany and failed to utter an apology for the bombing.

I don't think any decent, civilized person can look at pictures of Dresden after the bombing without being overcome by a sense of shock. The jagged ruins of walls emerging from fields of rubble, as far as the eye can see or the camera record, are a testament, of a kind, to human ingenuity. Only the long development of science and knowledge could have achieved this. As for the funeral pyres of bodies, piled up with their legs and arms emerging from the mass, or the corpses of the people boiled alive in the fountains in which they had taken refuge . . . one averts not only one's eyes but one's thoughts.

Yet the idea sometimes propounded by those who seek to condemn the bombing as an atrocity equal to, and counterbalancing, Nazi atrocities—that Dresden was some kind of city of the innocents, concerned only with the arts and having nothing to do with the war effort, cut off from and morally superior to the rest of Nazi Germany—is clearly absurd. It is in the nature of totalitarian regimes that no such innocence should persist anywhere; and it certainly didn't in Dresden in 1945. For example, the Zeiss-Ikon optical group alone employed 10,000 workers (and some forced labor), all engaged—of course—in war work. Nor had Dresden's record been very different from the rest of Germany's. Its synagogue was burned down during the orchestrated Kristallnacht of November 1938; the Gauleiter of Saxony, who had his seat in Dresden, was the notoriously brutal and corrupt Martin Mutschmann. The bombing saved the life of at least one man, the famous diarist Victor Klemperer, one of the 197 Jews still alive in the city (out of a former population of several thousand). He and the handful of remaining Jews had been marked down for deportation and death two days after the bombing; in the chaos after the bombing, he was able to escape and tear the yellow star from his coat.

Eighteen years after the end of the war, in 1963, the pro-Nazi historian David Irving published his first book, *The Destruction of Dresden*. In those days he was either less pro-Nazi than he later became or more circumspect—the memory of the war still being fresh—but it was probably not entirely a coincidence that he devoted his first attention to an event that Churchill suspected might be a blot on the British escutcheon. But Irving—later a leading Holocaust denier, who lost a famous libel suit against a historian who exposed him as such—clearly accepted in 1963 that there had been a Nazi genocide against the Jews, and he ended his book with an admission that the bombing (which he called "the biggest single massacre in European history") was "carried out in the cause of bringing to their knees a people who, corrupted by Nazism, had committed the greatest crimes against humanity in recorded time."

There were faint signs of Irving's later acceptance of the Nazi worldview in this book, though they probably went unnoticed at the time. Describing the state of medical services in Dresden after the bombing, he mentioned that "a vast euthanasia-hospital for mentally incurables" was transformed into a hospital for the wounded, without any remark upon the very concept of a "euthanasia-hospital for mentally incurables": an institution that by itself would be sufficient to negate one meaning of his ambiguous description of Dresden in a chapter heading as "The Virgin Target." (Did he mean that it had never yet been attacked, or that the city was an innocent virgin?)

Of course it would be absurd to pretend that the bombing of Dresden was conducted in order to put an end to the evil of its "euthanasia-hospital," however vast, or to rescue Victor Klemperer from certain death. Among other motives for bombing, no doubt, was the need to demonstrate to the advancing Russians the tremendous firepower of the West, despite its relative weakness in land armies.

Irving's book was influential, however, precisely because he hid, or had not yet fully developed, his Nazi sympathies. It achieved its greatest influence through *Slaughterhouse-Five*, Kurt Vonnegut's famous countercultural anti-war novel, published six years later, which makes grateful acknowledgment of Irving's book, whose inflated estimate of the death toll of the bombing it unquestioningly accepts. Vonnegut, an American soldier who was a prisoner of war in Dresden at the time of the bombing, having been captured during the land offensive in the west, writes of the war and the bombing itself as if it took place in no context, as if it were just an arbitrary and absurd quarrel between rivals, between Tweedledum and Tweedledee, with no internal content or moral meaning—a quarrel that nevertheless resulted in one of the rivals cruelly and thoughtlessly destroying a beautiful city of the other.

But Vonnegut, to whom it did not occur that his subject matter was uniquely unsuited to facetious, adolescent literary experimentation, was writing an anti-war tract in the form of a postmodern novel, not a historical reexamination of the bombing of Dresden or of Germany as a whole. The problem that has bedeviled any such reexamination is fear that sympathy for the victims, or regret that so much of aesthetic and cultural value was destroyed, might be taken as sympathy for Nazism itself. The difficulty of disentangling individual from collective responsibility for the evils perpetrated by the Nazi regime is unresolved even now, and perhaps is inherently unresolvable.

True, Hitler was immensely popular; on the other hand, he never won a majority of the votes in anything that resembled a free election, and public enthusiasm in dictatorships cannot be taken entirely at face value (in his diaries, Klemperer himself veers between thinking that most Germans were Nazis and that the enthusiasm was bogus and more or less forced). The Germans entered into the spirit of violence and denunciation with a will, but on the other hand intimidation was everywhere. A witness to the burning of the Dresden synagogue on Kristallnacht who was overheard publicly to liken it to the worst times of the Middle Ages was seized by the Gestapo and taken away: an object lesson to all those who saw or learned about his fate. And those who say that Nazism was the inevitable consummation of German history, inherent in all that had gone before, must explain why so many German Jews (my grandfather among them, a major in the imperial German army during the Great War) were deeply and patriotically attached to both the country and its culture, and why so many of them were so blind for so long. Their lack of foresight is surely as eloquent as the historian's hindsight.

By the end of the war, 600,000 Germans had been killed by the bombing campaign, and a third of the population rendered homeless. Yet when the war was over, none among the many millions affected could express his grief and despair openly, for to have done so would have rendered him open to the charge of Nazi sympathies. The East Germans could toll the bells for Dresden each anniversary of the bombing only because the government enforced the myth that all the Nazis originated from, and were now located in, West Germany. But normal, personal, unideological grief was not permitted.

W. G. Sebald, an expatriate German author who lived in England, where he died in a car crash in 2001, pointed out a curious lacuna in German literature of memoirs or fictional accounts of the bombing and its aftereffects. Millions suffered terribly, yet there is hardly a memoir or a novel to record it. Anything other than silence about what they experienced would have seemed, and still would seem, indecent and highly suspect, an attempt to establish a moral equivalence between the victims and perpetrators of Nazism.

Foreigners, such as the Swedish writer Stig Dagerman, could write about the sufferings of the Germans immediately after the war, but not the Germans themselves. Victor Gollancz, a British publisher of Polish-Jewish origin who could not be suspected in the slightest of Nazi sympathies and who had spent the entire 1930s publishing books warning the world of the Nazi peril, wrote and published a book in the immediate aftermath of the war called *In Darkest Germany*, in which he drew attention to the plight of the Germans living (and starving) among the ruins, which he observed on a visit there. To the charge that the Germans had brought it all on themselves and deserved no less, he replied with a three-word question: "And the children?" His book was furnished with many affecting pictures, perhaps the most poignant among them that of the comfortably attired Gollancz lifting the foot of a little German boy to demonstrate his pitiful footwear to the camera.

But for several decades it was impermissible for Germans to allude publicly to their own sufferings of the period, much of which must have been innocent, unless it be considered that all Germans were equally guilty ex officio, as it were. No doubt the impermissibility of publicly expressed complaint, and therefore of resentment, was a powerful stimulus of the *Wirtschaftswunder*, the economic miracle, into which the Germans in the West threw their potentially resentful energies after the war, for lack of anywhere else to direct them. But this left a legacy of deep emptiness that all the reflective Germans I have met seem to feel. Perhaps it explains also the German longing to travel, greater than that of any other nation I know.

In the last few years, best-selling books have begun to appear in Germany to record the suffering of the Germans during and after the war. Is this dangerous self-pity an implicit national self-exculpation? Or is it a sign of health, that at last Germans can approach their own past unencumbered by the psychological complexes bequeathed to them by their parents and grandparents?

As I walked through Dresden, I lamented the loss of an incomparable city, while thinking how difficult it must be to be a German, for whom neither memory nor amnesia can provide consolation.

2005

What the New Atheists Don't See

THE BRITISH PARLIAMENT'S first avowedly atheist member, Charles Bradlaugh, would stride into public meetings in the 1880s, take out his pocket watch, and challenge God to strike him dead in sixty seconds. God bided his time but got Bradlaugh in the end. A slightly later atheist, Bertrand Russell, was once asked what he would do if it proved that he was mistaken and if he met his maker in the hereafter. He would demand to know, Russell replied with all the high-pitched fervor of his pedantry, why God had not made the evidence of his existence plainer and more irrefutable. And Samuel Beckett came up with a memorable line: "God doesn't exist—the bastard!"

Beckett's wonderful outburst of disappointed rage suggests that it is not as easy as one might suppose to rid oneself of the notion of God. (Perhaps this is the time to declare that I am not myself a believer.) At the very least, Sartre's line implies that God's existence would solve some kind of problem—actually, a profound one: the transcendent purpose of human existence. Few of us, especially as we grow older, are entirely comfortable with the idea that life is full of sound and fury but signifies nothing. However much philosophers tell us that it is illogical to fear death, and that at worst it is only the process of dying that we should fear, people still fear death as much as ever. In like fashion, however many times philosophers say that it is up to us ourselves, and to no one else, to find the meaning of life, we continue to long for a transcendent purpose immanent in existence itself, independent of our own wills. To tell us that we should not feel this longing is a bit like telling someone in the first flush of love that the object of his affections is not worthy of them. The heart hath its reasons that reason knows not of.

Of course, men—that is to say, some men—have denied this truth ever since the Enlightenment, and have sought to find a way of life based entirely on reason. Far as I am from decrying reason, the attempt leads at best to Gradgrind and at worst to Stalin. Reason can never be the absolute dictator of man's mental or moral economy.

The search for the pure guiding light of reason, uncontaminated by human passion or metaphysical principles that go beyond all possible evidence, continues, however; and recently an epidemic rash of books has declared success, at least if success consists of having slain the inveterate enemy of reason, namely religion. The philosophers Daniel Dennett, A. C. Grayling, Michel Onfray, and Sam Harris, the biologist Richard Dawkins, and the journalist and critic Christopher Hitchens have all written books roundly condemning religion and its works. Evidently there is a tide in the affairs, if not of men, at least of authors.

The curious thing about these books is that the authors often appear to think they are saying something new and brave. They imagine themselves to be like the intrepid explorer Sir Richard Burton, who in 1853 disguised himself as a Muslim merchant, went to Mecca, and then wrote a book about his unprecedented feat. The public appears to agree, for the neo-atheist books have sold by the hundred thousand. Yet with the possible exception of Dennett's, they advance no argument that I, the village atheist, could not have made by the age of fourteen (Saint Anselm's ontological argument for God's existence gave me the greatest difficulty, but I had taken Hume to heart on the weakness of the argument from design).

I first doubted God's existence at about the age of nine. It was at the school assembly that I lost my faith. We had been given to understand that if we opened our eyes during prayers God would depart the assembly hall. I wanted to test this hypothesis. Surely, if I opened my eyes suddenly, I would glimpse the fleeing God? What I saw instead, it turned out, was the headmaster, Mr. Clinton, intoning the prayer with one eye closed and the other open, with which he beadily surveyed the children below for transgressions. I quickly concluded that Mr. Clinton did not believe what he said about the need to keep our eyes shut. And if he did not believe that, why should I believe in his God? In such illogical leaps do our beliefs often originate, to be disciplined later in life (if we receive enough education) by elaborate rationalization.

Dennett's *Breaking the Spell* is the least bad-tempered of the new atheist books, but it is deeply condescending to all religious people. Dennett argues that religion is explicable in evolutionary terms—for example, by our inborn human propensity, at one time valuable for our survival on the African savannahs, to attribute animate agency to threatening events.

For Dennett, to prove the biological origin of belief in God is to show its irrationality, to break its spell. But of course it is a necessary part of the argument that all possible human beliefs, including belief in evolution, must be explicable in precisely the same way; or else why single out religion for this treatment? Either we test ideas according to arguments in their favor, independent of their origins, thus making the argument from evolution irrelevant, or all possible beliefs come under the same suspicion of being only evolutionary adaptations—and thus biologically contingent rather than true or false. We find ourselves facing a version of the paradox of the Cretan liar: all beliefs, including this one, are the products of evolution, and all beliefs that are products of evolution cannot be known to be true.

One striking aspect of Dennett's book is his failure to avoid the language of purpose, intention, and ontological moral evaluation, despite his fierce opposition to teleological views of existence: the coyote's "methods of locomotion have been ruthlessly optimized for efficiency." Or: "The stinginess of Nature can be seen everywhere we look." Or again: "This is a good example of Mother Nature's stinginess in the final accounting combined with absurd profligacy in the methods." I could go on, but I hope the point is clear. (And Dennett is not alone in this difficulty: Michel Onfray's *Atheist Manifesto*, so rich in errors and inexactitudes that it would take a book as long as his to correct them, says on its second page that religion prevents mankind from facing up to "reality in all its naked cruelty." But how can reality have any moral quality without having an immanent or transcendent purpose?)

No doubt Dennett would reply that he is writing in metaphors for the layman and that he could translate all his statements into a language without either moral evaluation or purpose included in it. Perhaps he would argue that his language is evidence that the spell still has a hold over even him, the breaker of the spell for the rest of humanity. But I am not sure that this response would be psychologically accurate. I think Dennett's use of the language of evaluation and purpose is evidence of a deep-seated metaphysical belief (however caused) that Providence exists in the universe, a belief that few people, confronted by the mystery of beauty and of existence itself, escape entirely. At any rate, it ill behooves Dennett to condescend to those poor primitives who still have a religious or providential view of the world: a view that, at base, is no more refutable than Dennett's metaphysical faith in evolution.

Dennett is not the only new atheist to employ religious language. In *The God Delusion*, Richard Dawkins quotes with approval a new set of Ten Commandments for atheists, which he obtained from an atheist website, without considering odd the idea that atheists require commandments at all, let alone precisely ten of them; nor does their metaphysical status seem to worry him. The last of the atheist's Ten Commandments ends with the following: "Question everything." Everything? Including the need to question everything, and so on ad infinitum?

Not to belabor the point, but if I questioned whether George Washington died in 1799, I could spend a lifetime trying to prove it and find myself still, at the end of my efforts, having to make a leap, or perhaps several leaps, of faith in order to believe the rather banal fact that I had set out to prove. Metaphysics is like nature: though you throw it out with a pitchfork, it always returns. What is confounded here is surely the abstract right to question everything with the actual exercise of that right on all possible occasions. Anyone who did exercise his right on all possible occasions would wind up a short-lived fool.

This sloppiness and lack of intellectual scruple, with the assumption of certainty where there is none, combined with adolescent shrillness and intolerance, reach an apogee in Sam Harris's book *The End of Faith*. It is not easy to do justice to the book's nastiness; it makes Dawkins's claim that religious education constitutes child abuse look sane and moderate.

Harris tells us, for example, that "we must find our way to a time when faith, without evidence, disgraces anyone who would claim it. Given the present state of the world, there appears to be no other future worth wanting." I am glad that I am old enough that I shall not see the future of reason as laid down by Harris; but I am puzzled by the status of the compulsion in the first sentence that I have quoted. Is Harris writing of a historical inevitability? Of a categorical imperative? Or is he merely making a legislative proposal? This is who-will-rid-me-of-this-troublesome-priest language, ambiguous no doubt, but not open to a generous interpretation.

It becomes even more sinister when considered in conjunction with the following sentences, quite possibly the most disgraceful that I have read in a book by a man posing as a rationalist: "The link between belief and behavior raises the stakes considerably. Some propositions are so dangerous that it may be ethical to kill people for believing them. This may seem an extraordinary claim, but it merely enunciates an ordinary fact about the world in which we live."

Let us leave aside the metaphysical problems that these three sentences raise. For Harris, the most important question about genocide would seem to be: "Who is genociding whom?" To adapt Dostoevsky slightly, starting from universal reason I arrive at universal madness.

Lying not far beneath the surface of all the neo-atheist books is the kind of historiography that many of us adopted in our hormone-disturbed adolescence, furious at the discovery that our parents sometimes told lies and violated their own precepts and rules. It can be summed up in Christopher Hitchens's drumbeat in *God Is Not Great*: "Religion spoils everything."

What? The *Saint Matthew Passion*? The Cathedral of Chartres? The emblematic religious person in these books seems to be a Glasgow Airport bomber—a type unrepresentative of Muslims, let alone communicants of the poor old Church of England. It is surely not news, except to someone so ignorant that he probably wouldn't be interested in these books in the first place, that religious conflict has often been murderous and that religious people have committed hideous atrocities. But so have secularists and atheists, and though they have had less time to prove their mettle in this area, they have proved it amply. If religious belief is not synonymous with good behavior, neither is absence of belief, to put it mildly.

In fact, one can write the history of anything as a chronicle of crime and folly. Science and technology spoil everything: without trains and IG Farben, no Auschwitz; without transistor radios and mass-produced machetes, no Rwandan genocide. First you decide what you hate, and then you gather evidence for its hatefulness. Since man is a fallen creature (I use the term metaphorically rather than in its religious sense), there is always much to find.

The thinness of the new atheism is evident in its approach to our civilization, which until recently was religious to its core. To regret religion is, in fact, to regret our civilization and its monuments, its achievements, and its legacy. And in my own view, the absence of religious faith, provided that such faith is not murderously intolerant, can have a deleterious effect upon human character and personality. If you empty the world of purpose, make it one of brute fact alone, you empty it (for many people, at any rate) of reasons for gratitude, and a sense of gratitude is necessary for both happiness and decency. For what can soon, and all too easily, replace gratitude is a sense of entitlement. Without gratitude, it is hard to appreciate, or be satisfied with, what you have: and life will become an existential shopping spree that no product satisfies.

A few years back the National Gallery held an exhibition of Spanish still-life paintings. One of these paintings had a physical effect on the people who sauntered in, stopping them in their tracks; some even gasped. I have never seen an image have such an impact on people. The painting, by Juan Sánchez Cotán, now hangs in the San Diego Museum of Art. It showed four fruits and vegetables, two suspended by string, forming a parabola in a grey stone window.

Even if you did not know that Sánchez Cotán was a seventeenth-century Spanish priest, you could know that the painter was religious: for this picture is a visual testimony of gratitude for the beauty of those things that sustain us. Once you have seen it, and concentrated your attention on it, you will never take the existence of the humble cabbage—or of anything else—quite so much for granted, but will see its beauty and be thankful for it.

The painting is a permanent call to contemplation of the meaning of human life, and as such it arrested people who ordinarily were not, I suspect, much given to quiet contemplation.

The same holds true with the work of the great Dutch still life painters. On the neo-atheist view, the religious connection between Catholic Spain and Protestant Holland is one of conflict, war, and massacre only: and certainly one cannot deny this history. And yet something more exists. As with Sánchez Cotán, only a deep reverence, an ability not to take existence for granted, could turn a representation of a herring on a pewter plate into an object of transcendent beauty, worthy of serious reflection.

I recently had occasion to compare the writings of the neo-atheists with those of Anglican divines of the seventeenth and eighteenth centuries. I was visiting some friends at their country house in England, which had a library of old volumes; since the family of the previous owners had a churchman in every generation, many of the books were religious. In my own neo-atheist days I would have scorned these works as pertaining to a non-existent entity and containing nothing of value. I would have considered the authors deluded men, who probably sought to delude others for reasons that Marx might have enumerated.

But looking, say, into the works of Joseph Hall, D.D., I found myself moved: much more moved, it goes without saying, than by any of the books of the new atheists. Hall was bishop of Exeter and then of Norwich; though a moderate Puritan, he took the Royalist side in the English civil war and lost his see, dying in 1656 while Cromwell was still lord protector.

Except by specialists, Hall remains almost entirely forgotten today. I opened one of the volumes at random, his *Contemplations Upon the Principal Passages of the Holy Story*. Here was the contemplation on the sickness of Hezekiah:

> Hezekiah was freed from the siege of the Assyrians, but he is surprised with a disease. He, that delivered him from the hand

of his enemies, smites him with sickness. God doth not let us loose from all afflictions, when he redeems us from one.

To think that Hezekiah was either not thankful enough for his deliverance, or too much lifted up with the glory of so miraculous a favour, were an injurious misconstruction of the hand of God, and an uncharitable censure of a holy prince; for, though no flesh and blood can avoid the just desert of bodily punishment, yet God doth not always strike with an intuition of sin: sometimes he regards the benefit of our trial; sometimes, the glory of his mercy in our cure.

Hall surely means us to infer that whatever happens to us, however unpleasant, has a meaning and purpose; and this enables us to bear our sorrows with greater dignity and less suffering. And it is part of the existential reality of human life that we shall always need consolation, no matter what progress we make. Hall continues:

When, as yet, he had not so much as the comfort of a child to succeed him, thy prophet is sent to him, with the heavy message of his death: "Set thine house in order; for thou shalt die, and not live." It is no small mercy of God, that he gives us warning of our end. . . . No soul can want important affairs, to be ordered for a final dissolution.

This is the language not of rights and entitlements but of something much deeper—a universal respect for the condition of being human.

For Hall, life is instinct with meaning: a meaning capable of controlling man's pride at his good fortune and consoling him for his ill fortune. Here is an extract from Hall's *Characters of Virtues and Vices*:

He is an happy man, that hath learned to read himself, more than all books; and hath so taken out this lesson, that he can never forget it: that knows the world, and cares not for it; that, after many traverses of thoughts, is grown to know what he may trust to; and stands now equally armed for all events: that hath got the mastery at home; so as he can cross his will without a mutiny, and so please it that he makes it not a wanton: that, in earthly things, wishes no more than nature; in spiritual, is ever graciously ambitious: that, for his condition, stands on his own feet, not needing to lean upon the great; and can so frame his thoughts to his estate, that when he hath least, he cannot want, because he is as free from desire, as superfluity: that hath seasonably broken the headstrong restiness of prosperity; and can now manage it, at pleasure: upon whom, all smaller crosses light as hailstones upon a roof; and, for the greater calamities, he can take them as tributes of life and tokens of love; and, if his ship be tossed, yet he is sure his anchor is fast. If all the world were his, he could be no other than he is; no whit gladder of himself, no whit higher in his carriage; because he knows, that contentment lies not in the things he hath, but in the mind that values them.

Though eloquent, this appeal to moderation as the key to happiness is not original; but such moderation comes more naturally to the man who believes in something not merely higher than himself but higher than mankind. After all, the greatest enjoyment of the usages of this world, even to excess, might seem rational when the usages of this world are all that there is.

In his *Occasional Meditations*, Hall takes perfectly ordinary scenes—ordinary, of course, for his times—and derives meaning from them. Here is his meditation "Upon the Flies Gathering to a Galled Horse":

How these flies swarm to the galled part of this poor beast; and there sit, feeding upon that worst piece of his flesh, not meddling with the other sound parts of his skin! Even thus do malicious tongues of detractors: if a man have any infirmity in his person or actions, that they will be sure to gather unto, and dwell upon;

whereas, his commendable parts and well-deservings are passed by, without mention, without regard. It is an envious self-love and base cruelty, that causeth this ill disposition in men: in the mean time, this only they have gained; it must needs be a filthy creature, that feeds upon nothing but corruption.

Surely Hall is not suggesting (unlike Dennett in his unguarded moments) that the biological purpose of flies is to feed off injured horses, but rather that a sight in nature can be the occasion for us to reflect imaginatively on our morality. He is not raising a biological theory about flies, in contradistinction to the theory of evolution, but thinking morally about human existence. It is true that he would say that everything is part of God's Providence, but, again, this is no more (and no less) a metaphysical belief than the belief in natural selection as an all-explanatory principle.

Let us compare Hall's meditation "Upon the Sight of a Harlot Carted" with Harris's statement that some people ought perhaps to be killed for their beliefs:

With what noise, and tumult, and zeal of solemn justice, is this sin punished! The streets are not more full of beholders, than clamours. Every one strives to express his detestation of the fact, by some token of revenge: one casts mire, another water, another rotten eggs, upon the miserable offender. Neither, indeed, is she worthy of less: but, in the mean time, no man looks home to himself. It is no uncharity to say, that too many insult in this just punishment, who have deserved more. . . . Public sins have more shame; private may have more guilt. If the world cannot charge me of those, it is enough, that I can charge my soul of worse. Let others rejoice, in these public executions: let me pity the sins of others, and be humbled under the sense of my own.

Who sounds more charitable, more generous, more just, more profound, more honest, more humane: Sam Harris or Joseph Hall, D.D., late lord bishop of Exeter and of Norwich?

No doubt it helps that Hall lived at a time of sonorous prose, prose that merely because of its sonority resonates in our souls; prose of the kind that none of us, because of the time in which we live, could ever equal. But the style applies to the thought as well as the prose; and I prefer Hall's charity to Harris's intolerance.

2007

The Marriage of
Reason and Nightmare

◈ DESPITE unprecedented prosperity, we British are not as happy as we should be, at least if the causes of human happiness were mainly economic. It turns out, however, that ever-rising consumption is not the same thing as ever-greater contentment. Yet no one is quite sure what else is necessary. Anti-depressants in the water supply, perhaps? Urban life—and in the modern world, most life is urban—has an unpleasant edge in Britain, even in the midst of plenty. You hardly dare look a stranger in the eye, lest he take violent offense; the young, poor and prosperous alike, have imposed a curfew on the old after dark, and on everyone on Friday and Saturday nights; the age at which fellow citizens provoke fear declines constantly, so that one avoids even aggregations of eight-year-olds, as though they were piranhas in a jungle river.

The British state, for its part, is able to bully and regulate at will, thanks to technology—yet it seems to carry out these actions for their own sake, not for any higher purpose. The privatization of morality is so complete that no code of conduct is generally accepted, save that you should do what you can get away with; sufficient unto the day is the pleasure thereof. Nowhere in the developed world has civilization gone so fast and so far into reverse as here, at least to the extent to which civilization is made up of the small change and amenities of life.

No contemporary British writer captures our malaise better than does J. G. Ballard. In a writing career dating back half a century now, he has explored with acuity, from the aerie of his respectable suburban home outside London, the anxieties of modern existence—of what he calls the marriage of reason and nightmare. The reason is our technological advance, the nightmare the uses to which we have put it.

Much in Ballard's biography explains his sensitivity to aspects of modern decomposition that escape more superficial observers. But a biography cannot explain everything: as Pasteur once said, chance favors only a mind prepared. It is not only experience, therefore, but reflection upon it that makes the writer. A rich seam of ore is worthless without the will and ability to mine it.

Ballard's ore is his childhood. Born in Shanghai in 1930, the son of well-to-do British parents, he did not come to Britain until he was sixteen. The defining experience of his life, coloring all of his writing, was his internment by the Japanese, at thirteen, in a civilian camp during World War II. But it was not the internment alone that marked him; rather, it was the contrast with his earlier life. "Anyone who has experienced a war at first hand knows that it completely overturns every conventional idea of what makes up day-to-day reality," Ballard has observed. "You never feel quite the same again. It's like walking away from a plane crash; the world changes for you forever."

The protagonist of his autobiographical 1984 novel, *Empire of the Sun*, is Jim, a British boy also interned by the Japanese near Shanghai. Jim has led a privileged existence in a luxurious house with nine household servants, whom he knows not by name but by function or position, such as Amah, Number One Boy, and Number Two Boy. For Jim, the servants are not full human beings but animated objects whose purpose is to do his bidding. Neither especially good nor especially bad, rather a normal, thoughtless boy, he inherits the habit of command and takes his privileged way of life for granted. Not that he fails to notice the difference between his situation and that of most of the population around him; on the contrary, he is curious about life outside the European enclave. It is just that the difference for him is a brute fact about the constitution of the universe.

With the outbreak of war, everything changes. The Japanese sink a British ship and capture an American one, overthrowing the racial hierarchy. An amah slaps Jim in the face on no real provocation. He realizes suddenly two things about her that might have been evident earlier, had he stopped to think about them: first, that her life of constant labor has given her considerable strength; and second, that her previous passive obedience flowed neither from consent nor from lack of feeling but from fear, coercion, and an absence of alternatives. In that slap is concentrated all the resentment, humiliation, and hatred that an adult placed at the orders of a privileged and spoiled child comes to feel; and thus the Japanese victory is also an irreversible moral education for Jim. He will never again be able to conceive of the world as made solely for his convenience.

More than the racial hierarchy is overturned. In the struggle for survival that follows the Japanese occupation of Shanghai, Jim discovers many things: that civilized conduct is a veneer that unaccustomed hardship strips away; that previously prominent people can become insignificant under new conditions; that pride of race, of nation, of position are no protection against demoralization; that cruelty is common and self-sacrifice rare; in short, that everything he has assumed about the world is wrong.

In *Empire of the Sun*, Ballard describes childhood sights that must affect a person's outlook forever: "Fifty yards away the corpse of a young Chinese woman floated among the sampans, heels rotating around her head as if unsure in what direction to point that day." On the way to the camp where he will be interned, illness and death already striking down his fellow prisoners, Jim takes in his surroundings: "It seemed that the two missionary women on the floor were barely alive, with blanched lips and eyes like those of poisoned mice. Flies swarmed over their faces, darting in and out of their nostrils. . . . Their husbands sat side by side and stared at them in a resigned way, as if a taste for lying on the floor was a minor eccentricity shared by their wives."

Jim learns that the survival instinct easily trumps most forms of human solidarity. Desperate, his group of prisoners reaches a camp where a British official, evidently left some power and discretion, refuses them entry, fearing they will spread disease. They must seek another camp; more prisoners die on the way.

The internment camp in which Jim eventually finds himself fosters a horrifying loss of moral compunction, but it has its compensations. He forms an alliance of convenience with a young American, Basie, a small-time crook and wheeler-dealer of the kind that tends to do well in such situations. Ballard contrasts Basie with Jim's father, a stern and upright, if distant, figure. "At home, if he did anything wrong, the consequences seemed to overlay everything for days," Ballard writes. "With Basie they vanished instantly. For the first time in his life Jim felt free to do what he wanted."

In other words, the breakdown of the formalized social order, and its replacement with one based on more ruthless, informal, spontaneously generated rules, can liberate in a certain sense, in that it permits what was previously impermissible. In Freudian terms, the id escapes the power of the superego; what results both repels and attracts. This lesson Ballard never forgot.

Ballard arrived in England during the austere postwar years, the austerity lengthened by government policy that saw in it an opportunity for ideologically inspired social engineering. (Even now, one occasionally senses nostalgia in medical journals for the era of rationing, which imposed a scientifically approved diet on the population.) Ballard began medical school but dropped out after two years to become a writer. He never entirely lost his interest in medicine, however, and it is worth noting that doctors are important figures in his novels, the first of which came out in 1962.

All of Ballard's novels have a Robinson Crusoe theme: What happens to man when the props of civilization are removed from him, as they so easily are, by external circumstances or by the operation of his secret desires, or by both in concert? Ballard's past gave him an awareness of the fragility of things, even when they appear most solid; and in the introduction to his collected short stories, he tells us that he is "interested in the real future that I could see approaching." His method: extrapolate something—a trend, a feeling of dissatisfaction—that he detects in the present; magnify it; and then examine its consequences. He is a recorder of what he calls "the visionary present," a sociological Swift who claims (half-mistakenly, I think) that he does not write with a moral purpose but instead serves as "a scout who is sent on ahead to see if the water is drinkable or not."

In Ballard's earlier novels, the decomposition of society results largely from natural processes. For example, in his debut novel, *The Drowned World*, the earth has undergone an extremely rapid warming. (Ballard has an uncanny ability to anticipate future anxieties.) This warming, however, is the consequence not of man's activities but rather of huge sunspots. The sea has risen, flooding almost everything. London is under water, with only the upper heights of the taller buildings left above the surface. Most of the population has retreated to the cooler Arctic circle, while tropical vegetation has taken over the remaining landmasses; the fauna has begun swiftly to devolve to the Triassic era.

In these circumstances, it is not only the physical environment that changes, notes Dr. Bodkin, one of the book's characters.

"How often most of us have had the feeling of déjà vu, of having seen all this before, in fact of remembering these swamps and lagoons all too well," he points out. "However selective the conscious mind may be, most biological memories are unpleasant ones, echoes of danger and terror. Nothing endures for so long as fear." He adds: "Just as psychoanalysis reconstructs the original traumatic situation in order to release the repressed material, so we are now being plunged back into the archaeopsychic past, uncovering the ancient taboos and drives that have been dormant for epochs."

Later in Ballard's work, as in his 1973 novel *Concrete Island*, the cause of the regression to the primitive becomes manmade. "Soon after three o'clock on the afternoon of April 22nd 1973, a 35-year-old architect named Robert Maitland was driving down the high-speed exit lane in central London," the story begins. Maitland's car has a blowout at 70 miles per hour, and it plunges 30 yards down an embankment. Maitland finds himself in a small piece of wasteland, from which the only escape is up the embankment to the highway. He climbs up and tries to attract attention, but "his jacket and trousers were stained with sweat, mud and engine grease—few drivers, even if they did notice him, would be eager to give him a lift. Besides, it would be almost impossible to slow down here and stop. The pressure of the following traffic . . . forced them on relentlessly."

A passing taxi driver sees him and taps his head, signaling that Maitland must be mad. The castaway's situation is a vision of hell: "Horns blared endlessly as the three lines of vehicles, tail lights flaring, moved towards this junction. As Maitland stood weakly by the roadside, waving a feeble hand, it seemed to him that every vehicle in London had passed and re-passed him a dozen times, the drivers and passengers deliberately ignoring him in a vast spontaneous conspiracy." Trying to cross the highway, he is injured and thrown back down the embankment. He cannot escape from his desolate patch, isolated amid an agglomeration of millions of people. Now he must live by his wits, wresting from the wasteland whatever living he can.

It is significant that Maitland is an architect, for it is the architects, with their modernist dreams of making the world anew according to implacably abstract principles, who have created the wasteland in the first place. Ballard captures the socially isolating nature of modern architecture—and the modern way of life associated with it—with great symbolic force. The taxi driver, encased in his cage of pressed steel, can see in Maitland only a lunatic with whom he shares no humanity. The other drivers have lost their ability to choose: once on the road, they must inexorably move forward. They do not control the situation; the situation controls them. What should liberate—the car, with its theoretical ability to take you anywhere you want to go, whenever you want to go—becomes dehumanizing.

In the same year Ballard published his most controversial book, *Crash*, later made into an equally disturbing film by David Cronenberg. The book is a kind of visionary reductio ad absurdum of what Ballard sees as the lack of meaning in modern material abundance, in which erotic and violent sensationalism replace transcendent purpose: the book's characters speed to the sites of auto accidents to seek sexual congress with the dying bodies and torn metal. Ballard's method is Swift's, though with a less general target. To object that Ballard exaggerates the existential predicament of the modern middle classes is to miss the point, just as to object that Swift exaggerates man's absurdity, pretensions, and nastiness is to miss the point.

In his next book, *High-Rise*, published in 1975, Ballard sets a small civil war in a luxurious forty-story apartment building, where "the regime of trivial disputes and irritations . . . provided [the] only corporate life" of the two thousand inhabitants. Robert Laing is a doctor who is divorced, like all of Ballard's protagonists. "This over-priced cell, slotted almost at random into the cliff face of the apartment building, he had bought after his divorce specifically for its peace, quiet and anonymity," Ballard writes. It seems to be part of the modern condition that people find difficulty in living together, preferring an isolation in which human contact becomes superficial, fleeting, and primarily instrumental to immediate needs or desires.

Where people have few affective ties but nonetheless live together in close proximity, the potential for conflict is great. Though all the residents are well heeled, a version of class war breaks out in the high-rise, pitting the residents of the upper floors, who have paid the most for their apartments, against those of the lower floors. Boredom and a lack of common purpose provoke aggression, and self-destruction follows. Prosperity is not enough.

If anything, Ballard's vision has darkened. Twenty years after *High-Rise*, prosperity had increased enormously, and Ballard published *Cocaine Nights*, an attack on the very idea of the good life engendered by British consumer society. The novel is set in imaginary rich expatriate enclaves on the Spanish Mediterranean coast, towns "without either centre or suburbs, that seem to be little more than dispersal ground for golf courses and swimming pools." As one character says, "It's Europe's future. Everywhere will be like this soon."

The utter vacuity of the abundant life that the inhabitants have worked to achieve, enabling them to retire before fifty, is reflected in the enclaves' architecture and social atmosphere. "I looked down on an endless terrain of picture windows, patios and miniature pools," relates the protagonist, a travel writer.

Together they had a curiously calming effect, as if these residential compounds were a series of psychological pens that soothed and domesticated. . . . Nothing could ever happen in this affectless realm, where entropic drift calmed the surfaces of a thousand swimming pools.

Everywhere satellite dishes cupped the sky like begging bowls. The residents had retreated to their shady lounges, their bunkers with a view, needing only that part of the external world that was distilled from the sky by their satellite dishes.

The residents are refugees from a disordered world: "There's excellent security and not a trace of graffiti anywhere—most people's idea of paradise today." Freed from economic anxiety, they are also "refugees from time": in fact, they have "travelled to the far side of boredom" and are now "desperate for new vices."

A young tennis coach, Crawford, responsible for arranging the social life of the enclaves, hits on the idea of crime as the solution to the prevailing boredom. Unknowingly, he recapitulates the sociologist Émile Durkheim's view that criminals fulfill an important social function by providing the rest of the population with a cause for solidarity: for one can exercise solidarity only against something and somebody else. "How do you energize people, give them some sense of community?" Crawford asks. Politics is boring, religion too demanding. "Only one thing is left which can rouse people, threaten them directly and force them to act together. . . . Crime and transgressive behaviour. [They] provoke us and tap our need for strong emotion, quicken the nervous system and jump the synapses deadened by leisure and inaction." His conclusion: "A certain level of crime is part of the necessary roughage of life. Total security is a disease of deprivation."

By arranging for crimes to be committed at random, including a deliberate fire that kills five, Crawford brings the enclaves back to life, including cultural life. The residents start to play music and participate in theater productions. Instead of living in solipsistic isolation, they now meet regularly. Ballard is not suggesting that the immolation of people is a worthwhile price if only people take to the violin and footlights as a result. He is suggesting that, absent a transcendent purpose, material affluence is not sufficient—and may lead to boredom, perversity, and self-destruction.

In his two most recent novels, *Millennium People* and *Kingdom Come*, Ballard treats England as a country gripped by a consumerist fever, half aware that something more is necessary to lead a bearable human life, and thus vulnerable to an inchoate revolutionism whose inspiration is part fascist, part socialist. The books' characters are, as usual in Ballard, educated and middle class; no member of the underclass ever appears in his pages. This is not accidental. It is the educated class that is essential to running the country and that sets its moral tone; but "sheltered by benevolent shopping malls," Ballard writes in *Kingdom Come*, it "waits patiently for the nightmares that will wake [it] into a more passionate world." Believing in nothing, sated materially, it is capable of anything to escape boredom.

This represents an important insight. When I briefly served as a kind of vulgarity correspondent for a British newspaper—it sent me anywhere the British gathered to behave badly—I discovered to my surprise that the middle classes behaved in crowds with the same menacing disinhibition as their supposed social and educational inferiors. They swore and screamed abuse and made fascistic gestures and urinated in the street with the same abandon that they attributed to the proletarians. It was Ballard who first spotted that the bourgeoisie wanted to proletarianize itself without losing its economic privileges or political power.

In *Millennium People*, the residents of an affluent housing project called Chelsea Marina "had set about dismantling their middle-class world. They lit bonfires of books and paintings, educational toys and videos. . . . They had quietly discarded their world as if putting out their rubbish for collection. All over England an entire professional caste was rejecting everything it had worked so hard to secure."

This strikes me as a suggestive metaphor for much that has happened over the last four decades, not only in England (though especially here) but also throughout parts of Western society. We have become bored with what we have inherited, to which, for lack of talent, we have contributed so humiliatingly little. Ballard understands why educated people, haunted by the pointlessness of their lives, feel the need to protest, and he satirizes it in *Millennium People*. The book's protagonist, a psychologist, infiltrates the growing middle-class revolutionary movement and attends a protest against a cat show in a London exhibition hall with Angela, a revolutionary:

> Angela stared across the road with narrowed eyes and all a suburbanite's capacity for moral outrage. Walking around the exhibition two hours earlier, I was impressed by her unswerving commitment to the welfare of these luxurious pets. The protest rallies I had recently attended against globalisation, nuclear power and the World Bank were violent but well thought out. By contrast, this demonstration seemed endearingly Quixotic in its detachment from reality. I tried to point this out to Angela as we strolled along the line of cages.
>
> "Angela, they look so happy. . . . They're wonderfully cared for. We're trying to rescue them from heaven."
>
> Angela never varied her step. "How do you know?"
>
> "Just watch them." We stopped in front of a row of Abyssinians so deeply immersed in the luxury of being themselves that they barely noticed the admiring crowds. "They're not exactly unhappy. They'd be prowling around, trying to get out of the cages."
>
> "They're drugged." Angela's brows knotted. "No living creature should be caged. This isn't a cat show, it's a concentration camp."
>
> "Still, they are rather gorgeous."
>
> "They're bred for death, not life. The rest of the litter are drowned at birth. It's a vicious eugenic experiment, the sort of thing Dr. Mengele got up to."

The press not long ago ran obituaries of Peter Cadogan, whom one paper called a "professional protester." Another wrote that Cadogan "spent fifty years on a long quest of resistance to global injustices." He appeared inseparable from a megaphone, and no man would have been more disappointed to wake one day to a world denuded of injustice. Apparently, someone read the protest poems of William Blake to him on his deathbed, and these roused him temporarily from a coma. Protest was the meaning of his life. His dying words evoked Blake: "Live differently." Not better, but differently.

This mind-set can result in the violence from which, as Ballard discovered early in life, we are always but a hairbreadth away, however solidly founded our comfort may seem. Civilization's fragility does not make it unreal or valueless—quite the reverse. And while I suspect that Ballard would dislike seeing conservative implications drawn from his work, they are most certainly there.

2008

POLITICS
AND CULTURE

The Roads to Serfdom

PEOPLE IN BRITAIN who lived through World War II do not remember it with anything like the horror one might have expected. In fact they often remember it as the best time of their lives. Even allowing for the tendency of time to burnish unpleasant memories with a patina of romance, this is extraordinary. The war, after all, was a time of material shortage, terror, and loss: what could possibly have been good about it?

The answer, of course, is that it provided a powerful existential meaning and purpose. The population suffered at the hands of an easily identifiable external enemy, whose evil intentions it became the overriding purpose of the whole nation to thwart. A unified and preeminent national goal provided respite from the peacetime cacophony of complaint, bickering, and social division. And privation for a purpose brings its own content.

The war having instantaneously created a nostalgia for the sense of unity and transcendent purpose that prevailed in those years, the population naturally enough asked why such a mood could not persist into the peace that followed. Why couldn't the dedication of millions, centrally coordinated by the government—a coordinated dedication that had produced unprecedented quantities of aircraft and munitions—be adapted to defeat what London School of Economics head Sir William Beveridge, in his wartime report on social services that was to usher in the full-scale welfare state in Britain, called the "five giants on the road to reconstruction": Want, Disease, Ignorance, Squalor, and Idleness?

By the time Beveridge published his report in 1942, most of the intellectuals of the day assumed that the government, and only the government, could accomplish these desirable goals. Indeed, it all seemed so simple a matter that only the cupidity and stupidity of the rich could have prevented these ends from already having been achieved. The Beveridge Report states, for example, that want "could have been abolished in Britain before the present war" and that "the income available to the British people was ample for such a purpose." It was just a matter of dividing the national income cake into more equal slices by means of redistributive taxation. If the political will was there, the way was there; there was no need to worry about effects on wealth creation or any other adverse effects.

For George Orwell, writing a year before the Beveridge Report, matters were equally straightforward. "Socialism," he wrote, "is usually defined as 'common ownership of the means of production.' Crudely: the State, representing the whole nation, owns everything, and everyone is a state employee. . . . Socialism . . . can solve the problems of production and consumption. . . . The State simply calculates what goods will be needed and does its best to produce them. Production is only limited by the amount of labour and raw materials."

A few, equally simple measures would help bring about a better, more just and equitable society. Orwell recommended "i) Nationalisation of land, mines, railways, banks and major industries"; "ii) Limitation of incomes, on such a scale that the highest does not exceed the lowest by more than ten to one"; and "iii) Reform of the educational system along democratic lines." By this last, he meant the total prohibition of private education. He assumed that the culture, which he esteemed but which nevertheless was a product of the very system he so disliked, would take care of itself.

It would scarcely be an exaggeration to say that, by the time Orwell wrote, his collectivist philosophy was an intellectual orthodoxy from which hardly anyone in Britain would dare dissent, at least very strongly. "We are all socialists now," declared Bernard Shaw forty years before Orwell put forward his modest proposals. And before him, Oscar Wilde, in "The Soul of Man Under Socialism," accepted as incontrovertible—as not even worth supporting with evidence or argument, so obviously true was it—that poverty was the inescapable consequence of private property, and that one man's wealth was another man's destitution. And before Wilde, John Ruskin had argued, in *Unto This Last*, that a market in labor was both unnecessary and productive of misery. After all, he said, many wages were set according to an abstract (which is to say a moral) conception of the value of the job; so why should not all wages be set in the same way? Would this not avoid the unjust, irrational, and frequently harsh variations to which a labor market exposed people?

Ruskin was right that there are indeed jobs whose wages are fixed by an approximate notion of moral appropriateness. The salary of the president of the United States is not set according to the vagaries of the labor market; nor would the number of candidates for the post change much if it were halved or doubled. But if every wage in the United States were fixed in the same way, wages would soon cease to mean very much. The economy would be demonetized, the impersonal medium of money being replaced in the allocation of goods and services by personal influence and political connection—precisely what happened in the Soviet Union. Every economic transaction would become an expression of political power.

The growing spirit of collectivism in Britain during the war provoked an Austrian economist who had taken refuge there, Friedrich A. von Hayek, to write a polemical counterblast to the trend: *The Road to Serfdom*, published in 1944. It went through six printings in its first year, but its effect on majority opinion was, for many years to come, negligible. Hayek believed that while intellectuals in modern liberal democracies—those to whom he somewhat contemptuously referred as the professional secondhand dealers in ideas—did not usually have direct access to power, the theories they diffused among the population ultimately had a profound, even determining, influence upon their society. Intellectuals are of far greater importance than appears at first sight.

Hayek was therefore alarmed at the general acceptance of collectivist arguments—or worse still, assumptions—by British intellectuals of all classes. He had seen the process—or thought he had seen it—before, in the German-speaking world from which he came, and he feared that Britain would likewise slide down the totalitarian path. Moreover, at the time he wrote, the "success" of the two major totalitarian powers in Europe, Nazi Germany and Soviet Russia, seemed to have justified the belief that a plan was necessary to coordinate human activity toward a consciously chosen goal. For George Orwell, the difference between the two tyrannies was one of ends, not of means: he held up Nazi Germany as an exemplar of economic efficiency resulting from central planning, but he deplored the ends that efficiency accomplished. While the idea behind Nazism was "human inequality, the superiority of Germans to all other races, the right of Germany to rule the world," socialism (of which, of course, the Soviet Union was the only exemplar at the time) "aims, ultimately, at a world-state of free and equal human beings." Same means, different ends: but Orwell, at this point in his intellectual development, saw nothing intrinsically objectionable in the means themselves, or that they must inevitably lead to tyranny and oppression, independently of the ends for which they were deployed.

Against the collectivists, Hayek brought powerful—and to my mind obvious—arguments that, however, were scarcely new or original. Nevertheless, it is often, perhaps usually, more im-

portant to remind people of old truths than to introduce them
to new ones.

Hayek pointed out that the wartime unity of purpose was
atypical; in more normal times, people had a far greater, indeed
an infinite, variety of ends, and anyone with the power to adju-
dicate among them in the name of a conscious overall national
plan, allowing a few but forbidding most, would exert vastly
more power than the most bloated plutocrat of socialist propaganda had ever done in a free-market society.

Orwell's assertion that the state would simply calculate what
was needed airily overlooked the difficulties of the matter, as
well as his proposal's implications for freedom. The "directing
brains," as Orwell called them, would have to decide how many
hairpins, how many shoelaces were "needed" by the population
under their purview. They would have to make untold millions
of such decisions, likewise coordinating the production of all
components of each product, on the basis of their own arbitrary
notions of what their fellow citizens needed. Orwell's goal,
therefore, was a society in which the authorities strictly rationed
everything; for him, and untold intellectuals like him, only rationing was rational. It takes little effort of the imagination to
see what this control would mean for the exercise of liberty.
Among other things, people would have to be assigned work regardless of their own preferences.

Collectivist thinking arose, according to Hayek, from impatience, a lack of historical perspective, and an arrogant belief
that, because we have made so much technological progress,
everything must be susceptible to human control. While we take
material advance for granted as soon as it occurs, we consider
remaining social problems as unprecedented and anomalous,
and we propose solutions that actually make more difficult further progress of the very kind that we have forgotten ever happened. While everyone saw the misery the Great Depression
caused, for example, few realized that, even so, living standards

actually continued to rise for the majority. If we live entirely in the moment, as if the world were created exactly as we now find it, we are almost bound to propose solutions that bring even worse problems in their wake.

In reaction to the unemployment rampant in what W. H. Auden called "the low dishonest decade" before the war, the Beveridge Report suggested that it was government's function to maximize security of income and employment. This proposition was bound to appeal strongly to people who remembered mass unemployment and collapsing wages; but however high-minded and generous it might have sounded, it was wrong. Hayek pointed out that you can't give everyone a job irrespective of demand without sparking severe inflation. And you can no more protect one group of workers' wages against market fluctuations without penalizing another group than you can discriminate positively in one group's favor without discriminating negatively against another. This is so, and it is beyond any individual human's control that it should be so. Therefore no amount of planning would ever make Beveridge's goals possible, however desirable they might be in the abstract.

But just because a goal is logically impossible to achieve does not mean that it must be without effect on human affairs. As the history of the twentieth century demonstrates perhaps better than any other, impossible goals have had at least as great an effect on human existence as more limited and possible ones.

The most interesting aspect of Hayek's book, however, is not his refutation of collectivist ideas—which, necessary as it might have been at that moment, was not by any means original. Rather, it is his observations of the moral and psychological effects of the collectivist ideal that, sixty years later, capture the imagination—mine, at least.

Hayek thought he had observed an important change in the character of the British people, as a result both of their collectivist aspirations and of such collectivist measures as had already been legislated. He noted, for example, a shift in the locus of people's moral concern. Increasingly it was the state of society or the world as a whole that engaged their moral passion, not their own conduct. "It is, however, more than doubtful whether a fifty years' approach towards collectivism has raised our moral standards, or whether the change has not rather been in the opposite direction," he wrote. "Though we are in the habit of priding ourselves on our more sensitive social conscience, it is by no means clear that this is justified by the practice of our individual conduct." In fact, "It may even be . . . that the passion for collective action is a way in which we now without compunction collectively indulge in that selfishness which as individuals we had learnt a little to restrain."

Thus, to take a trifling instance, it is the duty of the city council to keep the streets clean; therefore my own conduct in this regard is morally irrelevant—which no doubt explains why so many young Britons now leave a trail of litter behind them wherever they go. If the streets are filthy, it is the council's fault. Indeed, if anything is wrong—for example, my unhealthy diet—it is someone else's fault, and the job of the public power to correct. Hayek—with the perspective of a foreigner who had adopted England as his home—could perceive a further tendency that has become much more pronounced since then: "There is one aspect of the change in moral values brought about by the advance of collectivism which at the present time provides special food for thought. It is that the virtues which are held less and less in esteem and which consequently become rarer are precisely those on which the British people justly prided themselves and in which they were generally agreed to excel. The virtues possessed by the British people in a higher degree than most other people . . . were independence and self-reliance, individual initiative and local responsibility . . . non-interference with one's neighbour and tolerance of the different and queer, respect for custom and tradition, and a healthy suspicion of power and authority."

He might have added the sense of irony, and therefore of the inherent limitations of human existence, that was once so prevalent, and that once protected the British population from infatuation with utopian dreams and unrealistic expectations. And the virtues that Hayek saw in them—the virtues immortalized in the pages of Jane Austen and Charles Dickens—were precisely the virtues that my mother and her cousin also saw when they first arrived in Britain as refugees from Germany in 1938. Orwell saw (and valued) them too, but unlike Hayek he did not ask himself where they came from; he must have supposed that they were an indestructible national essence, distilled not from history but from geography.

The British are sadly changed from Hayek's description of them. A sense of irony is the first victim of utopian dreams. The British tolerance of eccentricity has also evaporated; uniformity is what they want now, and are prepared informally to impose. They tolerate no deviation in taste or appearance from themselves: and certainly in the lower reaches of society, people who are markedly different, either in appearance because of the vagaries of nature, or in behavior because of an unusual taste they may have, especially for cultivation, meet with merciless ridicule, bullying, and even physical attack. It is as if people believed that uniformity of appearance, taste, and behavior were a justification of their own lives, and any deviation an implied reproach or even a declaration of hostility. A young patient of mine, who disliked the noise, the vulgarity, and the undertone of violence of the nightclubs where her classmates spent their Friday and Saturday nights, was derided and mocked into conformity: it was too hard to hold out. The pressure to conform to the canons of popular taste—or rather, lack of taste—has never been stronger. Those without interest in soccer hardly dare mention it in public, for fear of being considered enemies of the people. A dispiriting uniformity of character, deeply shallow, has settled over a land once richer in eccentrics than any other. No more Edward Lears for us: we prefer notoriety to oddity now.

The British are no longer sturdily independent as individuals, either, and now feel no shame or even unease, as not long ago they would have felt, in accepting government handouts. Indeed, 40 percent of them now receive such handouts: for example, the parents of every child are entitled not merely to a tax reduction but to an actual payment in cash, no matter the state of their finances. As for those who, though able-bodied and perfectly able to work, are completely dependent on the state for their income, they unashamedly call the day when their welfare checks arrive "payday." Between work and parasitism they see no difference. "I'm getting paid today," they say, having not only accepted but thoroughly internalized the doctrine propounded in the Beveridge Report, that it is the duty of the state to assure everyone of a decent minimum standard of life regardless of his conduct. The fact of having drawn sixteen breaths a minute, twenty-four hours a day, is sufficient to entitle each of them to his minimum; and oddly enough, Hayek saw no danger in this and even endorsed the idea. He did not see that to guarantee a decent minimum standard of life would demoralize not only those who accepted it but those who worked in the more menial occupations, and whose wages would almost inevitably give them a standard of living scarcely higher than that of the decent minimum provided merely for drawing breath.

In any case, Hayek did not quite understand the source of the collectivist rot in Britain. It is true, of course, that an individualist society needs a free, or at least a free-ish, market; but a necessary condition is not a sufficient one. It is not surprising, though, that Hayek should have emphasized the danger of a centrally planned economy when so prominent a figure as Orwell—who was a genuine friend of personal liberty, who valued the peculiarities of English life, and who wrote movingly about such national eccentricities as a taste for racy seaside postcards and a love of public school stories—should so little have understood the preconditions of English personal liberty that he wrote, only three years before Hayek's book was published: "The liberty of the individual is still believed in, almost as in the nineteenth century. But this has nothing to do with economic liberty, the right to exploit others for profit."

It is depressing to see a man like Orwell equating profit with exploitation. And it is certainly true that Britain after the war took no heed of Hayek and for a time seemed bent on state control of what were then called "the commanding heights of the economy." Not only did the Labour government nationalize health care, but also coal mining, electricity and gas supply, the railways and public transportation (including the airlines), telecommunications, and even most of the car industry. Yet at no time could it remotely be said that Britain was slipping down the totalitarian path.

The real danger was far more insidious, and Hayek incompletely understood it. The destruction of the British character did not come from Nazi- or Soviet-style nationalization or centralized planning, as Hayek believed it would. For collectivism proved to be not nearly as incompatible with, or diametrically opposed to, a free, or free-ish, market as he had supposed.

In fact, Hilaire Belloc, in his book *The Servile State*, predicted just such a form of collectivism as early as 1912. Like most intellectuals of the age, Belloc was a critic of capitalism because he held it responsible for the poverty and misery he saw in the London slums. His view was static, not dynamic: he did not see that the striving there could—and would—lift people out of their poverty, and he therefore argued that the liberal, laissez-faire state—"mere capitalist anarchy," he called it—could not, and should not, continue. He foresaw three possible outcomes.

His preferred resolution was more or less the same as Carlyle's half a century earlier: a return to the allegedly stable and happy medieval world of reciprocal rights and duties. There would be guilds of craftsmen and merchants in the towns, supplying mainly handmade goods to one another and to peasant farmers, who in turn would supply them with food. Everyone would own at least some property, thereby having a measure of independence, but no one would be either plutocrat or pauper. However desirable this resolution, though, even Belloc knew it was fantasy.

The second possible resolution was the socialist one: total expropriation of the means of production, followed by state ownership, allegedly administered in the interests of everyone. Belloc had little to say on whether he thought this would work, since in his opinion it was unlikely to happen: the current owners of the means of production were still far too strong.

That left the third, and most likely, resolution. The effect of collectivist thought on a capitalist society would not be socialism but something quite distinct, whose outlines he believed he discerned in the newly established compulsory unemployment insurance. The means of production would remain in private hands, but the state would offer workers certain benefits in return for their quiescence and agreement not to agitate for total expropriation as demanded in socialist propaganda.

Unlike Orwell or Beveridge, however, Belloc realized that such benefits would exact a further price: "A man has been compelled by law to put aside sums from his wages as insurance against unemployment. But he is no longer the judge of how such sums shall be used. They are not in his possession; they are not even in the hands of some society which he can really control. They are in the hands of a Government official. 'Here is work offered to you at twenty-five shillings a week. If you do not take it you shall certainly not have a right to the money you have been compelled to put aside. If you will take it the sum shall stand to your credit, and when next in my judgment your unemployment is not due to your recalcitrance and refusal to labour, I will permit you to have some of your money; not otherwise.'"

What applied to unemployment insurance would apply to all other spheres into which government intruded, Belloc intuited; and all of the benefits government conferred, paid for by the compulsory contributions of the taxpayer, in effect would take choice and decision-making out of the hands of the individual, placing them in those of the official. Although the benefits offered by the government were as yet few when Belloc wrote, he foresaw a state in which the "whole of labour is mapped out and controlled." In his view, "The future of industrial society, and in particular of English society . . . is a future in which subsistence and security shall be guaranteed for the Proletariat, but shall be guaranteed . . . by the establishment of that Proletariat in a status really, though not nominally, servile." The people lose "that tradition of . . . freedom, and are most powerfully inclined to [the] acceptance of [their servile status] by the positive benefits it confers."

And this is precisely what has happened to the large proportion of the British population that has been made dependent on the welfare state.

The state action that was supposed to lead to the elimination of Beveridge's five giants of Want, Disease, Ignorance, Squalor, and Idleness has left many people in contemporary Britain with very little of importance to decide for themselves, even in their own private spheres. They are educated by the state (at least nominally), as are their children in turn; the state provides for them in old age and has made saving unnecessary or, in some cases, actually uneconomic; they are treated and cured by the state when they are ill; they are housed by the state if they cannot otherwise afford decent housing. Their choices concern only sex and shopping.

No wonder the British have changed in character, their sturdy independence replaced with passivity, querulousness, or even, at the lower reaches of society, a sullen resentment that not enough has been or is being done for them. For those at the bottom, such money as they receive is, in effect, pocket money, like the money children get from their parents, reserved for the satisfaction of whims. As a result, they are infantilized. If they behave irresponsibly—for example, by abandoning their own children wherever they father them—it is because both the rewards for behaving responsibly and the penalties for behaving irresponsibly have vanished. Such people come to live in a limbo, in which there is nothing much to hope or strive for and nothing much to fear or lose. Private property and consumerism coexist with collectivism, and freedom for many people now means little more than choice among goods. The free market, as Hayek did not foresee, has flourished alongside the collectivism that was—and, after years of propaganda, still is—justified by the need to eliminate the five giants. For most of the British population today, the notion that people could solve many of the problems of society without governmental *Gleichschaltung*, the Nazi term for overall coordination, is completely alien.

Of course, the majority of Britons are still not direct dependents of the state. "Only" about a third of them are: the 25 percent of the working population who are public employees (the government has increased them by nearly one million since 1997, no doubt in order to boost its election chances); and the 8 percent of the adult population either unemployed or registered as disabled, and thus utterly dependent on government handouts. But the state looms large in all our lives, not only in its intrusions but in our thoughts: for so thoroughly have we drunk at the wells of collectivism that we see the state always as the solution to any problem, never as an obstacle to be overcome. One can gauge how completely collectivism has entered our soul—so that we are now a people of the government, for the government, by the government—by a strange but characteristic British locution. When, on the rare occasions that our chancellor of the exchequer reduces a tax, he is said to have "given money away." In other words, all money is his, and whatever we have in our pockets is what he, by grace and favor, has allowed us.

Our Father, which art in Downing Street. . . .

2005

How Not to Do It

NOT LONG AGO the British government announced—because the opposition in Parliament forced it to announce—that seventy prisoners, including three murderers and an unspecified number of burglars, drug dealers, and holders of false passports, had escaped from a single minimum-security prison in one year alone. Twenty-eight of them were still at large.

That so many of them absconded suggested that they were not quite the reformed characters that justified lower levels of security in the first place; but as usual in Britain, temporary embarrassment soon subsides into deep amnesia. The fact is that the whole episode is precisely what we have come to expect of our public administration and was nothing out of the ordinary.

In the same week my former colleagues, senior doctors in the hospital that I worked in until my recent retirement, received a leaflet with their monthly pay stubs. It offered them, along with all other employees, literacy training: a little late in their careers as doctors, one might have thought.

The senior doctors could take up to thirty hours of free courses to improve their literacy and numeracy skills, all in working time, of course. In these courses, they could learn to spell at least some words, to punctuate, to add and do fractions, and to read a graph.

"Do you have a SPIKEY [*sic*] profile?" asked the leaflet, and went on to explain: "A spikey profile is when a person is good at literacy but not at mathematics or visa [*sic*] versa." The reader could address himself to one of no fewer than four members of the hospital staff who were "contact persons" for the courses, among them the vocational training coordinator and the nonvocational training coordinator. In case none was available to answer the telephone or reply to e-mails, the reader could contact one of three central government agencies that deal with the problem of illiterate and innumerate employees.

Here, truly, was a case of the lunatics taking over the asylum; but there is more to the ignorance and incompetence pervading the leaflet than meets the eye. Such ignorance and incompetence are now so systematic and widespread in the British public service that if they are not the result of deliberate policy, they might as well be. In fact there is now a profoundly catalytic relationship between the intellectual, moral, and economic corruption of the British public service and the degeneration of the national character. Which among all the various factors came first and is therefore ultimately causative is not easy to say; as usual, I suspect that intellectual error is at the root of most evil. But why such error should have found so ready an acceptance raises the specter of an infinite regress of explanation, which perhaps we can avoid only by invoking a dialectical approach.

Three recent books give us an insight into the nature of the corruption that has sprung from the ever-wider extension of self-arrogated government responsibility in Britain, and they shed light as well on the effect that government expansion has upon the population. By the time you have finished reading them, you are unsure as to whether Gogol, Kafka, or Orwell offers the best insight into contemporary British reality. Gogol captures the absurdity all right, and Kafka the anxiety caused by an awareness of sinister but unidentifiable forces behind what is happening; but you also need Orwell to appreciate, and sometimes even to admire, the brazenness with which officialdom twists language to mean the opposite of what it would once ordinarily have meant.

Two of the books are by men who work in the front line of the public service, one in law enforcement and the other in education. Like me, they write pseudonymously. By describing their day-to-day routine, Police Constable David Copperfield and teacher Frank Chalk show how the British state now works, or rather operates, with devastating effect on the British character.

Copperfield, whose website is so annoying to politicians in power that they feel obliged to denigrate it in Parliament, and whose book is titled *Wasting Police Time*, is an ordinary constable in an ordinary British town. As he makes clear in his book, very little of his time at work is spent in activity that could deter crime, discover those who commit it, or bring them to justice. His induction into the culture of politically correct bureaucratic incompetence was immediate on joining up: he had naively supposed that the main purpose of his job was the protection of the public by the suppression of malefaction, instead of which he discovered that it was to "set about changing the racist, homophobic and male-dominated world in which we lived." The first three days of his training were about prejudice and discrimination—in short, "diversity training." There never was to be any training in the mere investigation of crimes, a minor and secondary part of modern police work in Britain.

The mandated, politically inspired obsession with racism is on view in the crawlingly embarrassing and condescending speech that the deputy chief constable (deputy police chief) of North Wales, Clive Wolfendale, gave to the inaugural meeting of the North Wales Black Police Association. He decided, Copperfield reports, to speak to the black officers in rap verse, which is about as tactful as addressing Nelson Mandela in pidgin. Here is an extract from Wolfendale's speech:

Put away your cameras and your notepads for a spell.

I got a story that I really need to tell.

Bein' in the dibble [police] is no cakewalk when you're black.

125

If you don't get fitted, then you'll prob'ly get the sack.
You're better chillin' lie down and just be passive.
No place for us just yet in the Colwyn Bay Massive [police force].

That must have encouraged the black officers no end: if the (white) deputy chief constable, in his maladroit attempt to demonstrate sympathy with them, had called them a bunch of jungle bunnies, he could hardly have made his feelings clearer. His speech reveals what I have long suspected: that anti-racism is the new racism.

It is also, and simultaneously, a job opportunity and work-avoidance scheme. Copperfield recounts how, in 1999, a police officer said to a black motorist who did not answer a question, "Okay, so you're deaf as well as black." The report of the official inquiry into the subsequent complaint had 62 pages of attachments, 20 pages of witness statements, and 172 pages of interview transcripts. Legal and disciplinary proceedings took 19 months to complete.

Meanwhile, as the police devote vast energies (and expenditures) to such incidents, crimes such as street robbery and assault continue their inexorable rise and turn much of the country into a no-go area for all but the drunk or the violently inclined.

Copperfield, who joined the police full of idealism, soon notices (as how could he not?) that the completion of bureaucratic procedure is now more important to the police than anything else. All is in order if the forms are filled in correctly. A single arrest takes up to six hours to process, so many and various are the forms. He notices that there are more nonpolice employed in his police station than uniformed officers; and of the latter, the majority are deskbound. The station parking lot is full nine to five, Monday through Friday, but the whole town has only three or four officers to patrol the streets—in cars, of course, not on foot.

The author describes the intellectual and moral corruption that all this bureaucracy brings in its wake. Take, for example, the so-called administrative detection, which allows the police and their political masters to mislead the public about the seriousness and efficiency with which the authorities tackle criminality. It works something like this: someone calls the police about a trifling dispute—one neighbor accuses the other of threatening behavior, say, and the accused then in turn accuses the accuser. The cops record the two complaints as crimes and take statements from every possible witness. This, of course, can take a very long time, because by the time cops arrive, the witnesses will probably have dispersed. They have to be traced and contacted, and—because the police are now so touchingly-feelingly sensitive to the wishes of the public—mutually convenient times must be arranged for the taking of statements.

When finally the police have gathered all the information, they write it up; but of course, no prosecution follows, because by then the complainants have withdrawn their complaint, and in any case the prosecuting authorities would regard the whole business as too trivial to be worth a trial. But the two crimes go into the records as having been solved. And since the politicians in charge judge police performance by the proportion of crimes the force solves, cops do not devote attention to most real crimes, in which detection is difficult and very uncertain of success.

The uselessness of a police force that once excited the admiration of the world is now taken for granted by every Briton who calls the police only to obtain a crime number for insurance purposes, not in the expectation or even hope of any effort at detection. This is not because the individual policeman is lazy, ill intentioned, corrupt, or stupid, though in the present system he might just as well be: for the system in which he works imposes upon him all the effects (or defects) of precisely those qualities. P. C. Copperfield is clearly a man who wants to do a good job, like most of the policemen I have met, but the system actively and deliberately prevents him from doing so.

I happened, while waiting to interview a man in prison, to be reading Copperfield's book, and two plainclothes policemen in the waiting room saw it. They had read the work, and I asked them whether what Copperfield wrote was true. "Every word," they replied.

Frank Chalk's book *It's Your Time You're Wasting* tells essentially the same story, this time with regard to education. It surely requires some explanation that, in a country that expends $5,200 a year for eleven years on each child's education, a fifth of children leave school virtually unable to read or write, let alone do simple arithmetic. It takes considerable organization to achieve so little, especially when the means by which practically all children can be taught to read to a high standard are perfectly well known. A small local educational authority in Scotland, for example, West Dumbarton, has virtually eliminated illiteracy in children, despite the fact that its population is among the poorest in Scotland, by using simple teaching methods and at an additional cost of precisely $25 per pupil.

The intellectual corruption of the English education system is near complete (the Scottish system is rather better). For example, there is a government inspectorate of schools, charged with the maintenance of standards. But it gives each school it visits several weeks' warning of an impending inspection, ample time for even the dullest-witted school administrators to construct a Potemkin village. And then it criticizes all the wrong things: the inspectors criticized Frank Chalk, for example, for having imposed discipline upon his class and thereby having impeded the spontaneity and creativity of the children—which, in the circumstances of the slum school in which he teaches, they principally express in vandalism. The school inspectorate therefore appears to believe in the truth of the anarchist Bakunin's dictum—that the destructive urge is also creative.

As an epigraph to his book, Chalk quotes the British deputy prime minister, John Prescott. In that great man's immortal words, which tell you everything about the caliber of the British government that you really need to know, "If you set up a school and it becomes a good school, the great danger is that everyone wants to go there." And that would never do.

In the looking-glass world of modern British public administration, nothing succeeds like failure, because failure provides work for yet more functionaries and confers an ever more providential role upon the government. A child who does not learn to read properly often behaves badly in school and thus becomes the subject (or is it object?) of inquiries by educational psychologists and social workers. As Chalk describes, they always find that the child in question lacks self-esteem and therefore should be allowed to attend only those classes that he feels he can cope with. The so-called senior management team in the school— teachers who have retired into a largely administrative role— deals with all disciplinary problems by means of appeasement, for lack of any other permissible method available to them.

A perverse ideology reigns, in which truth and probity play no part. When grading the children's work, Chalk is expected to make only favorable comments, designed to boost egos rather than improve performance. Public examinations are no longer intended to test educational attainment against an invariant standard but to provide the government with statistics that give evidence of ever-better results. In pursuit of such excellence, not only do examinations require ever less of the children, but so-called course work, which may actually be done by the children's parents or even by the teachers themselves, plays an important part in the marks the children receive—and it is marked by the very teachers whose performance is judged by the marks that their pupils achieve. The result, of course, is a swamp of corruption. Wading through it, teachers become utterly cynical, time-serving, and without self-respect.

A perfect emblem of the Gogolian, Kafkaesque, and Orwellian nature of the British public administration is the term "social inclusion" as applied in the educational field. Schools may no longer exclude disruptive children—that would be the very opposite of social inclusion—so a handful of such children may render quite pointless hundreds or even thousands of hours of schooling for scores or even hundreds of their peers who, as a result, are less likely to succeed in life. Teachers such as Chalk are forced to teach mixed-ability classes, which can include the mentally handicapped (their special schools having been closed in the name of social inclusion). The most intelligent children in the class fidget with boredom while the teacher persistently struggles to instill understanding in the minds of the least intelligent children of what the intelligent pupils long ago grasped. The intelligent are not taught what they could learn, while the unintelligent are taught what they cannot learn. The result is chaos, resentment, disaffection, and despair all round.

Britain now has more educational bureaucrats than teachers, as well as more health-service administrators than hospital beds. No self-evident or entirely predictable failure, no catastrophe they have brought about at the behest of their political masters ever affects their careers, in part because they move from post to post so quickly that none of them ever gets held responsible for anything. The public hospital in which my wife worked as a doctor before her recent retirement built a $28 million extension, but what had been imperatively necessary for the health of the town's population six years ago became equally superfluous four years later and had to be closed down with great urgency, though with the public assurances of the bureaucrats then in charge that they were "passionately" committed to the townspeople's welfare. No one, of course, was ever held responsible for this expensive fiasco, which fully partook of the absurdity Gogol portrays, the menace Kafka evokes (employees were, on the whole, too frightened for their careers to speak out), and the mendacity Orwell dramatizes.

Insight into why expensive failure is so vitally necessary to the British government—or indeed, to any government once it arrogates responsibility for almost everything, from the national diet to the way people think—glimmers out from management consultant David Craig's recent book, *Plundering the Public Sector*. Craig catalogs what at first sight seems the almost incredible incompetence of the British government in its efforts to "modernize" the public administration. For example, not a single large-scale information technology project instituted by the government has worked. The National Health Service has spent $60 billion on a unified information technology system, no part of which actually functions. Projects routinely get canceled after $400 to $500 million has been spent on them. Modernization in Britain's public sector means delay and inefficiency procured at colossal expense.

How is this to be explained? I learned a very good lesson when, twenty years ago, I worked in Tanzania. This well-endowed and beautiful country was broken down and economically destitute to a shocking degree. A shard of mirror was a treasured possession; a day's wages bought a man one egg on the open market. It was quicker to go to Europe than to telephone it. Nothing, not even the most basic commodity such as soap or salt, was available to most of the population.

At first, I considered that the president, Julius Nyerere, who was so revered in "progressive" circles as being halfway between Jesus Christ and Mao Tse-tung, was a total incompetent. How could he reconcile the state of the country with his rhetoric of economic development and prosperity for everyone? Had he no eyes to see, no ears to hear?

But then the thought dawned on me, admittedly with embarrassing slowness, that a man who had been in power virtually unopposed for nearly a quarter of a century could not be called incompetent, once one abandons the preposterous premise that he was trying to achieve what he said he was trying to achieve. As a means of remaining in power, what method could be better than to have an all-powerful single political party distribute economic favors in conditions of general shortage? That explained how, and why, in a country of the involuntarily slender, the party officials were fat. This was not incompetence; it was competence of a very high order. Unfortunately it was very bad for the population as a whole.

The scheme in Britain is, of course, rather different. (It is not necessary to believe that such schemes have been consciously elaborated, incidentally; rather, they are inherent in the statism that comes naturally to so many politicians because of their self-importance.) The hoops that bind the government to the consultants who advise it in its perennially failing schemes of modernization are those of gold. As Craig demonstrates (though without understanding all the implications), the consultants need failure in Britain to perpetuate the contracts that allow them to charge so outrageously and virtually ad libitum (Craig suggests that $140 billion has disappeared so far, with no end in sight); and, in turn, the government benefits from having this rich but utterly dependent clientele.

The beauty of the system is that dependence on expensive failure reaches quite low levels of the administration: for example, all those "civilians" (as nonpolice workers for the police are called) in P. C. Copperfield's police station, as well as the educational psychologists whom Frank Chalk derides. The state has become a vast and intricate system of patronage, whose influence very few can entirely escape. It is essentially corporatist: the central government, avid for power, sets itself up as an authority on everything and claims to be omnicompetent both morally and in practice; and by means of taxation, licensing, regulation, and bureaucracy, it destroys the independence of all organizations that intervene between it and the individual citizen. If it can draw enough citizens into dependence on it, the central government can remain in power, if not forever, then for a very long time, at least until a crisis or cataclysm forces change.

At the very end of the chain of patronage in the British state is the underclass, who (to change the metaphor slightly) form the scavengers or bottom-feeders of the whole corporatist ecosystem. Impoverished and degraded as they might be, they are nonetheless essential to the whole system, for their existence provides an ideological proof of the necessity of providential government in the first place, as well as justifying many employment opportunities in themselves. Both Copperfield and Chalk describe with great eloquence precisely what I have seen myself in this most wretched stratum of society: large numbers of people corrupted to the very fiber of their being by having been deprived of responsibility, purpose, and self-respect, void of hope and fear alike, living in as near to purgatory as anywhere in modern society can come.

Of course the corporatist system, at least in its British incarnation, is a house of cards, or perhaps a better analogy would be with a pyramid scheme. Hundreds of thousands of people are employed to perform tasks that are not merely useless but actually obstructive of real work and economically counterproductive. The bureaucracy insinuates itself into the smallest cracks of daily life. Renting out a house recently, I learned from a real estate agent that the government sends inspectors, in the guise of prospective tenants, to check that the upholstery on chairs is fire-retardant. The inspectors have no other function. The regulations shift like one of those speeded-up meteorological maps on television, creating the need for yet more inspections and inspectors. Recent new regulations for landlords exceed one thousand pages of close print; in the meantime, Britain does not remain short of decaying housing stock while rents are among the highest in the world.

The government has to pay for all this activity, supposedly carried out on behalf of the population, somehow. It is simultaneously committed to huge public expenditure and apparent, though not real, control of the public debt. It reconciles the irreconcilable by not including the extravagantly generous pension obligations of the public service in its debt calculations—pension obligations that, properly accounted for, now amount to nearly 56 percent of GDP. Also not included is the government's increasing resort to private finance of government institutions, which involves huge future expenditure obligations without the capital costs having to appear in the national accounts.

In other words, the government has turned the cynical last words of an eighteenth-century absolute monarch, Louis XV, into the guiding principle of its policy: *après nous, le déluge.*

2007

A Prophetic and
Violent Masterpiece

◈ WHEN, as a medical student, I emerged from the cinema having watched Stanley Kubrick's controversial film of *A Clockwork Orange*, I was astonished and horrified to see a group of young men outside dressed up as droogs, the story's adolescent thugs who delighted in what they called "ultra-violence."

The film had been controversial in Britain; its detractors, who wanted it banned, charged that it glamorized and thereby promoted violence. The young men dressed as droogs seemed to confirm the charge, though of course it is one thing to imitate a form of dress and quite another to imitate behavior. Still, even a merely sartorial identification with psychopathic violence shocked me, for it implied an imaginative sympathy with such violence; and seeing those young men outside the theater was my first intimation that art, literature, and ideas might have profound—and not necessarily favorable—social consequences. A year later, a group of young men raped a seventeen-year-old girl in Britain as they sang "Singin' in the Rain," a real-life replay of one of the film's most notorious scenes.

The author of the book, Anthony Burgess, a polymath who once wrote five novels in a year, came to dislike this particular work intensely, not because of any practical harm to society that the film version of it might have caused but because he did not want to go down in literary history as the author of a book made famous, or notorious, by a movie. Irrespective of the value of his other work, however, *A Clockwork Orange* remains a novel of immense power. Linguistically inventive, socially prophetic, and philosophically profound, it comes very close to being a work of genius.

The story, set in the England of the near future (the book was published in 1962), is simple. The narrator, Alex, a precocious fifteen-year-old psychopath who has no feeling for others, leads a small gang in many acts of gratuitous, and much enjoyed, violence. Eventually, caught after a murder, he goes to prison, where—after another murder—the authorities offer to release him if he submits to a form of aversive conditioning against violence called the Ludovico Method. On his release, however, he attempts suicide by jumping out of a window, receiving a head injury that undoes his conditioning against violence. Once more he becomes the leader of a gang.

In the final chapter of the book's British version, Alex again rejects violence, this time because he discovers within himself, spontaneously, a source of human tenderness that makes him want to settle down and have a baby. In the American edition—which Stanley Kubrick used—this last chapter is missing: Alex is not redeemed a second time, but returns, apparently once and for all, to the enjoyment of arbitrary and anti-social violence. In this instance it is the British who were the optimists and the Americans the pessimists: Burgess's American publisher, wanting the book to end unhappily, omitted the last chapter.

Burgess had been a schoolteacher (like William Golding, author of *Lord of the Flies*) and evidently sensed a stirring of revolt among the youth of his country and elsewhere in the West, a revolt with which—as a deeply unconventional man who felt himself to be an outsider, however wealthy or famous he became, and who drank deep at the well of resentment as well as of spirituous liquors—he felt some sympathy and might even have helped in a small way to foment. And yet, as a man who was also deeply steeped in literary culture and tradition, he understood the importance of the shift of cultural authority from the old to the young and was very far from sanguine about its effects. He thought that the shift would lead to a hell on earth and the destruction of all that he valued.

He marks the separateness of his novel's young protagonists from their elders by their adoption of a new argot as well as a new form of dress. Vital for groups antagonistic toward the dominant society around them, such argots allow them to identify and communicate with insiders and exclude outsiders. Although I worked in a prison for fourteen years, for example, I never came to understand the language that prisoners used as they shouted to one another across landings and between buildings. It was their means of resisting domination. In the French *banlieues, les jeunes* use an argot derived from words spelled and pronounced backward—and completely incomprehensible to educated speakers of French. People of Jamaican descent in Britain use a patois when they want not to be understood by anyone else. The connection between argot and criminal purposes has long been close, of course; and the importance that Burgess ascribes to the new argot in *A Clockwork Orange* suggests that he saw youthful revolt as an expression more of self-indulgence and criminality than of idealism—the latter, shallower view becoming orthodoxy among intellectuals not long after *A Clockwork Orange* appeared.

Burgess's creation of a completely convincing new argot more or less ex nihilo is an extraordinary achievement. *Nadsat* (Russian for "teen"), as its speakers call it, is a mixture of anglicized Russian words—particularly provocative at the height of the cold war—and Cockney rhyming slang. As a linguistic invention, it is the equal of Orwell's Newspeak. Alex, the narrator, though cold-blooded and self-centered, is intelligent and expresses himself with great force. A vocabulary that is entirely

new and incomprehensible at the beginning of the book becomes so thoroughly familiar to the reader at the end that he
forgets he has ever had to learn its meaning: it seems completely
natural after only a hundred pages. On the very first page, when
Alex describes his gang's intention to do a robbery, he says:

[T]here was no real need . . . of crasting [robbing] any more
pretty polly [money] to tolchock [hit] some old veck [man] in
an alley and viddy [see] him swim in his blood while we
counted the takings and divided by four, nor to do the ultra-vi-
olent on some shivering starry [old] grey-haired ptitsa [woman]
in a shop and go smecking [laughing] off with the till's guts.

Of course, the lack of real "need" does not prevent Alex and
his gang from robbing in a cruel and violent way, for their cruelty and violence is an end in itself, joyfully engaged in. Not for
Burgess was the orthodox liberal view that economic deprivation and lack of opportunity cause crime.

The gang's solipsistic and dehumanizing argot reflects this
cold-bloodedness. Sexual intercourse, for example, becomes
"the old in-out-in-out," a term without reference to the other
participant, who is merely an object. The gang attacks a schoolteacher carrying books home from the library, for no reason
other than a free-floating malevolence and joy in cruelty:

Pete held his rookers [hands] and Georgie sort of hooked his
rot [mouth] wide open for him and Dim yanked out his false
zoobies [teeth], upper and lower. He threw these down on the
pavement and then I treated them to the old boot-crush, though
they were hard bastards like. . . . The old veck [man] began to
make sort of chumbling shooms [sounds]—"wuf waf wof"—so
Georgie let go of holding his goobers [jaws] apart and just let
him have one in the toothless rot with his ringy fist, and that
made the old veck start moaning a lot then, then out comes the
blood, my brothers, real beautiful.

I doubt that a lack of feeling for others has ever been expressed more powerfully.

Burgess intuited with almost prophetic acuity both the nature and characteristics of youth culture when left to its own devices, and the kind of society that might result when that culture became predominant. For example, adults grow afraid of the young and defer to them, something that has certainly come to pass in Britain, where adults now routinely look away as youngsters commit anti-social acts in public, for fear of being knifed if they do otherwise, and mothers anxiously and deferentially ask their petulant five-year-old children what they would like to eat, in the hope of averting tantrums. The result is that adolescents and young men take any refusal of a request as lèse-majesté, a challenge to the integrity of their ego. When I refused to prescribe medicine that young men wanted but that I thought they did not need, they would sometimes answer in aggrieved disbelief, "No? What do you mean, no?" It was not a familiar concept. And in a sense, my refusal was pointless, insofar as any such young man would soon enough find a doctor whom he could intimidate into prescribing what he wanted. Burgess would not have been surprised by this state of affairs: he saw it coming.

When Alex and his gang enter a pub—they are underage, but no one dares challenge them—they spread fear by their mere presence.

> Now we were the very good malchicks [boys], smiling good evensong to one and all, though these wrinkled old lighters [people] started to get all shook, their veiny old rookers all trembling round their glasses, and making the suds [drink] spill on the table. "Leave us be, lads," said one of them, her face all mappy with being a thousand years old, "we're only poor old women."

Intimidation of the aged and contempt for age itself are an essential part of the youth culture: no wonder aging rock stars are eternal adolescents, wrinkled and arthritic but trapped in the poses of youth. Age for them means nothing but indignity.

Alex's parents (one of the things Burgess didn't foresee is the rise of the single-parent family) are afraid of him. He comes home late and plays his music very loud, but "Pee and em [Father and Mother] . . . had learnt now not to knock on the wall with complaints of what they called noise. I had taught them. Now they would take sleep-pills." When Alex's father wants to know what he does at night—recall that Alex is only fifteen—he is apologetic and deferential: "'Not that I want to pry, son, but where exactly is it you go to work of evenings?' . . . My dad was like humble mumble chumble. 'Sorry, son,' he said. 'But I get worried sometimes.'"

When in a symbolic reversal of the direction of authority Alex offers his father some money (robbed, of course) so that he can buy himself a drink in the pub, his father says: "Thanks, son. . . . But we don't go out much now. We daren't go out much, the streets being what they are. Young hooligans and so on. Still, thanks."

In 1962 the idea that the young would someday impose upon old people in Britain a de facto after-dark curfew was still unimaginable, but Burgess, seeing the cloud no bigger than a man's hand on the horizon, imagined that outcome very vividly. With a prophet's imagination, he saw what would happen when the cloud grew until it covered the sky.

With like prescience, Burgess foresaw many other aspects of the youth culture to come: the importance that mind-altering drugs and an industrialized pop music would play in it, for example. (Burgess did not, however, suggest that high culture was necessarily ennobling in itself. Alex, much superior in intelligence to his followers, is a devotee of classical music, listening to which, however, increases his urge to commit violence. No doubt Burgess had in mind those Nazis who could listen with emotion to Schubert lieder after a hard day's genocide.)

Burgess foresaw the importance that the youth culture would attach to sexual precocity and a kind of disabused knowingness. In a remarkable rape scene, Alex meets two ten-year-old girls who, like him, are skipping school, in a record shop, where they are listening to pop music with suggestive titles such as "Night After Day After Night."

> They saw themselves, you could see, as real grown-up devotchkas [girls] already, what with the old hipswing when they saw your Faithful Narrator, brothers, and padded groodies [breasts] and red all ploshed on their goobers [lips]. . . . [T]hey viddied [saw] themselves as real sophistoes. . . . They had the same ideas or lack of, and the same color hair—a like dyed strawy. Well, they would grow up real today. . . . No school this afterlunch, but education certain, Alex as teacher.

Their education that afternoon consists of repeated rape by an already experienced fifteen-year-old.

It would not have surprised Burgess that magazines for ten- or eleven-year-old girls are now filled with advice about how to make themselves sexually attractive, that girls of six or seven are dressed by their single mothers in costumes redolent of prostitution, or that there has been a compression of generations, so that friendships are possible between fourteen- and twenty-six-year-olds. The precocity necessary to avoid humiliation by peers prevents young people from maturing further and leaves them in a state of petrified adolescence. Convinced that they already know all that is necessary, they are disabused about everything, for fear of appearing naive. With no deeper interests, they are prey to gusts of hysterical and childish enthusiasm; only increasingly extreme sensation can arouse them from their mental torpor. Hence the epidemic of self-destructiveness that has followed in the wake of the youth culture.

The world in which youth culture predominates and precocity is the highest achievement is one in which all tenderness is absent. When Alex and his gang attack the teacher, they find a letter in his pocket, which one of them reads out derisively: "My darling one . . . I shall be thinking of you while you are away and hope you will remember to wrap up warm when you go out at night."

Such simple and heartfelt affection and concern for another person are extinct in the world of Alex and his droogs. Alex is incapable of putting himself in the place of anyone else, of "changing places in fancy with the sufferer," as Adam Smith puts it. Self-absorbed, he is self-pitying but has no pity for others. When he is arrested after the brutal murder of an old woman, he calls the policemen who have arrested him "bullies" and accuses them when they laugh at him of "the heighth of . . . callousness." Alex is quite incapable of connecting his own savage behavior with the words that he applies to the police. I was reminded of a case of murder in which I gave testimony recently: the young murderer kicked his girlfriend's head so hard that he broke her jaw in many places and forced her tongue through the back of her throat, and her stomach filled with blood—and a neighbor heard him laugh as he kicked. A policeman, after listening to his lies and evasions for two days, accused him of having no remorse for his deed. "You 'ave no feelings," the murderer rejoined. "I pity your poor wife"—just like Alex in *A Clockwork Orange*, but without the intelligence and the taste for classical music.

In the world of Alex and his droogs, all relations with other human beings are instrumental means to a selfish, brutal, hedonistic end. And this is the world that so many of my patients now inhabit, a world in which perhaps a third of the British population lives. It is also the world in which having a baby is the fulfillment of a personal human right, and nothing else.

But Burgess was not merely a social and cultural prophet. *A Clockwork Orange* grapples as well with the question of the origin and nature of good and evil. The Ludovico Method that

Alex undergoes in prison as a means of turning him into a model citizen in exchange for his release is in essence a form of conditioning. Injected with a drug that induces nausea, Alex must then watch films of the kind of violence that he himself committed, his head and eyelids held so that he cannot escape the images by looking away from them—all this to the piped-in accompaniment of the classical music he loves. Before long such violence, either in imagery or in reality, as well as the sound of classical music, causes him nausea and vomiting even without the injection, as a conditioned response. Alex learns to turn the other cheek, as a Christian should: when he is insulted, threatened, or even struck, he does not retaliate. After the treatment—at least, until he suffers his head injury—he can do no other.

Two scientists, Drs. Branom and Brodsky, are in charge of the "treatment." The minister of the interior, responsible for cutting crime in a society now besieged by the youth culture, says: "The Government cannot be concerned any longer with outmoded penological theories. . . . Common criminals . . . can best be dealt with on a purely curative basis. Kill the criminal reflex, that's all." In other words, a criminal or violent act is, in essence, no different from the act of a rat in a cage, who presses a lever in order to obtain a pellet of food. If you shock the rat with electricity when it presses the lever instead of rewarding it with food, it will soon cease to press the lever. Criminality can be dealt with, or "cured," in the same way.

At the time Burgess wrote *A Clockwork Orange*, doctors were trying to "cure" homosexuals by injecting them with apomorphine, a nausea-inducing drug, while showing them pictures of male nudes. And overwhelmingly, the dominant school of psychology worldwide at the time was the behaviorism of Harvard professor B. F. Skinner. His was what one might call a "black box" psychology: scientists measured the stimulus and the response but exhibited no interest whatsoever in what happened between the two, as being intrinsically immeasurable and therefore unknowable. While Skinner might have quibbled about the details of the Ludovico Method (for example, that Alex got the injection at the wrong time in relation to the violent films that he had to watch), he would not have rejected its scientific—or rather, scientistic—philosophy.

In 1971, the very year in which the Kubrick film of *A Clockwork Orange* was released, Skinner published a book entitled *Beyond Freedom and Dignity*. He sneered at the possibility that reflection upon our own personal experience and on history might be a valuable source of guidance to us in our attempts to govern our lives. "What we need," he wrote, "is a technology of behavior." Fortunately one was at hand. "A technology of operant behavior is . . . already well advanced, and it may prove commensurate with our problems." As he put it, "[a] scientific analysis shifts the credit as well as the blame [for a man's behavior] to the environment." What goes on in a man's mind is quite irrelevant; indeed, "mind," says Skinner, is "an explanatory fiction."

For Skinner, being good is behaving well; and whether a man behaves well or badly depends solely upon the schedule of reinforcement that he has experienced in the past, not upon anything that goes on in his mind. It follows that there is no new situation in a man's life that requires conscious reflection if he is to resolve the dilemma or make the choices that the new situation poses: for everything is merely a replay of the past, generalized to meet the new situation.

The Ludovico Method, then, was not a far-fetched invention of Burgess's but a simplified version—perhaps a reductio ad absurdum, or ad nauseam—of the technique for solving all human problems that the dominant school of psychology at the time suggested. Burgess was a lapsed Catholic, but he remained deeply influenced by Catholic thought throughout his life. The Skinnerian view of man appalled him. He thought that a human being whose behavior was simply the expression of conditioned responses was not fully human but an automaton. If he did the right thing merely in the way that Pavlov's dog salivated at the sound of a bell, he could not be a good man: indeed, if all his behavior was determined in the same way, he was hardly a man at all. A good man, in Burgess's view, had to have the ability to do evil as well as good, an ability that he would voluntarily restrain, at whatever disadvantage to himself.

Being a novelist rather than an essayist, however, and a man of many equivocations, Burgess put these thoughts in *A Clockwork Orange* into the mouth of a ridiculous figure, the prison chaplain, who objects to the Ludovico Method—but not enough to resign his position, for he is eager to advance in what Alex calls "Prison religion." Burgess puts the defense of the traditional view of morality as requiring the exercise of free will— the view that there is no good act without the possibility of a bad one—into the mouth of a careerist.

The two endings of *A Clockwork Orange*—the one that Burgess himself wrote and the truncated one that his American publisher wanted and that Kubrick used for his film—have very different meanings.

According to the American-Kubrick version, Alex resumes his life as a violent gang leader after his head injury undoes the influence of the Ludovico Method. He returns to what he was before, once more able to listen to classical music (Beethoven's Ninth) and fantasize violence without any conditioned nausea:

> Oh, it was gorgeosity and yumyumyum. When it came to the Scherzo I could viddy myself very clear running and running on like very light and mysterious nogas [feet], carving the whole litso [face] of the creeching [screaming] world with my cut-throat britva [razor]. And there was the slow movement and the lovely last singing movement still to come. I was cured all right.

Kubrick even suggests that this is a happy outcome: better an authentic psychopath than a conditioned, and therefore inauthentic, goody-goody. Authenticity and self-direction are thus made to be the highest goods, regardless of how they are expressed. And this, at least in Britain, has become a prevailing orthodoxy among the young. If, as I have done, you ask the aggressive young drunks who congregate by the thousand in every British town or city on a Saturday night why they do so, or British soccer fans why they conduct themselves so menacingly, they will reply that they are expressing themselves, as if there were nothing further to be said on the matter.

The full, British version of *A Clockwork Orange* ends very differently. Alex begins to lose his taste for violence spontaneously, when he sees a happy, normal couple in a café, one of whom is a former associate of his. Thereafter, Alex begins to imagine a different life for himself and to fantasize a life that includes tenderness:

> There was Your Humble Narrator Alex coming home from work to a good hot plate of dinner, and there was this ptitsa [girl] all welcoming and greeting like loving. . . . I had this sudden very strong idea that if I walked into the room next to this room where the fire was burning away and my hot dinner laid on the table, there I should find what I really wanted. . . . For in that other room in a cot was laying gurgling goo goo goo my son. . . . I knew what was happening, O my brothers. I was like growing up.

Burgess obviously prefers a reformation that comes spontaneously from within, as it does in the last chapter, to one that comes from without, by application of the Ludovico Method. Here he would agree with Kubrick—an internal reformation is more authentic, and thus better in itself because it is a true expression of the individual. Perhaps Burgess also believes that such an internal reformation is likely to go deeper and be less susceptible to sudden reversal than reformation brought from outside.

Burgess also suggests the somewhat comforting message, at odds with all that has gone before, that Alex's violence is nothing new in the world and that the transformation of immature, violent, and solipsistic young men into mature, peaceful, and considerate older men will continue forever, as it has done in the past, because deep inside there is a well of goodness, man having been born with original virtue rather than original sin (this is the Pelagian heresy, to which Burgess admitted that he was attracted). There is a never-ending cycle:

> [Y]outh is only being in a way like it might be an animal. No, it is not just like being an animal so much as being like one of these malenky [small] toys you viddy being sold in the streets, like little chellovecks [men] made out of tin and with a spring inside and then a winding handle on the outside and you wind it up grrr grrr grrr and off it itties [goes], like walking, O my brothers. But it itties in a straight line and bangs straight into things bang bang and it cannot help what it is doing. Being young is like being like one of these malenky machines.
>
> My son, my son. When I had my son I would explain all that to him when he was starry [old] enough to like understand. But then I knew he would not understand or would not want to understand at all and would do all the veshches [things] I had done . . . and I would not be able to really stop him. And nor would he be able to stop his own son, brothers. And so it would itty on to like the end of the world.

And this, surely, is partly right. Four centuries ago Shakespeare wrote:

> I would there were no age between sixteen and three-and-twenty, or that youth would sleep out the rest; for there is nothing in the between but getting wenches with child, wronging the ancientry, stealing, fighting.

And certainly it is true that criminality, statistically speaking, is an activity of the young and that there are few prisoners in the prison in which I worked who had been incarcerated for a crime committed after age thirty-five. There seems to be a biological dimension to garden-variety wrongdoing.

But a quietistic message—cheerful insofar as it implies that violence among young men is but a passing phase of their life and that the current era is no worse in this respect than any past age, and pessimistic in the sense that a reduction of the overall level of violence is impossible—is greatly at odds with the socially prophetic aspect of the book, which repeatedly warns that the coming new youth culture, shallow and worthless, will be unprecedentedly violent and anti-social. And of Britain, at least, Burgess was certainly right. He extrapolated from what he saw in the prime manifestation of the emerging youth culture, pop music, to a future in which self-control had shrunk to vanishing, and he realized that the result could only be a Hobbesian world, in which personal and childish whim was the only authority to guide action. Like all prophets, he extrapolated to the nth degree; but a brief residence in a British slum should persuade anyone that he was not altogether wide of the mark.

A Clockwork Orange is not completely coherent. If youth is violent because the young are like "malenky machines" who cannot help themselves, what becomes of the free will that Burgess otherwise saw as the precondition of morality? Do people grow into free will from a state of automatism, and, if so, how and when? And if violence is only a passing phase, why should the youth of one age be much more violent than the youth of another? How do we achieve goodness, both on an individual and social level, without resort to the crude behaviorism of the Ludovico Method or any other form of cruelty? Can we bypass consciousness and reflection in our struggle to behave well?

There are no schematic answers in the book. One cannot condemn a novel of 150 pages for failing to answer some of the most difficult and puzzling questions of human existence, but one can praise it for raising them in a peculiarly profound manner and forcing us to think about them. To have combined this with acute social prophecy (to say nothing of entertainment) is genius.

2006

It's This Bad

◆ RETURNING BRIEFLY to England from France for a speaking engagement, I bought three of the major dailies to catch up on the latest developments in my native land. The impression they gave was of a country in the grip of a thoroughgoing moral frivolity. In a strange inversion of proper priorities, important matters are taken lightly and trivial ones taken seriously.

This is not the charming or uplifting frivolity of Feydeau's farces or Oscar Wilde's comedies; it is the frivolity of real decadence, bespeaking a profound failure of nerve bound to have disastrous consequences for the country's quality of life. The newspapers portrayed frivolity without gaiety and earnestness without seriousness—a most unattractive combination.

Of the two instances of serious matters taken with levity, the first concerned a forty-two-year-old barrister, Peter Wareing, attacked in the street while walking home from a barbecue with two friends, a man and a woman. They passed a group of seven teenagers who had been drinking heavily, one of whom, a girl, complained that the barrister and his friends were "staring" at them. Nowadays, English youth of aggressive disposition and porcelain-fragile ego regard such alleged staring as a justified casus belli.

The girl attacked the woman in the other party. When Wareing and his male friend tried to separate them, two of the youths, aged eighteen and sixteen, in turn attacked them. They hit the barrister's friend into some bushes, injuring him slightly, and then knocked the barrister to the ground, knocking him down a second time after he had struggled to his feet. This second time, his head hit the ground, injuring his brain severely. He was unconscious and on life support for two months afterward. At first, his face was so disfigured that his three children were not allowed to see him.

The doctors told his wife, a nurse, that he was unlikely to survive, and she prepared the children for their father's death. She wrote in a journal that she kept as she sat by his bed, "Very scary feeling that all his natural life is gone." Nevertheless he made an unexpected, though partial, recovery. His memory remains impaired, as does his speech; he may never be able to resume his legal career fully. It is possible that his income will be much lower for the rest of his life than it would otherwise have been, to the great disadvantage of his wife and children.

One of the two assailants, Daniel Hayward, demonstrated that he had learned nothing—at least, nothing of any comfort to the public—after he had ruined the barrister's life. While awaiting trial on bail, he attacked the landlord of a pub and punched him in the face, for which he received a sentence of twenty-one days in prison.

Before passing sentence for the attack on Wareing, the judge was eloquent in his condemnation of the two youths. "You were looking for trouble and prepared to use any excuse to visit violence on anyone you came by. It is the callousness of this that is so chilling. . . . You do not seem to care that others have been blighted by your gratuitous violence."

You might have thought that this was a prelude to the passing of a very long prison sentence on the two youths. If so, however, you would be entirely mistaken. Both received sentences of eighteen months, with an automatic nine-month remission, more or less as of right. In other words, they would serve nine months in prison for having destroyed the health and career of a completely innocent man, caused his wife untold suffering, and deprived three young children of a normal father. One of the perpetrators, too, had shown a complete lack of remorse for what he had done and an inclination to repeat it.

Even at so young an age, nine months is not a very long time. Moreover, when I recall that for youths like these a prison sentence is likely to be a badge of honor rather than a disgrace, I cannot but conclude that the British state is either utterly indifferent to or incapable of the one task that inescapably belongs to it: preserving the peace and ensuring that its citizens may go about their lawful business in safety. It does not know how to deter, prevent, or punish. The remarks of the policeman in charge of the case were not encouraging. He said afterward that he hoped "the sentences . . . send a clear warning to people who think it is acceptable to consume large quantities of alcohol, then assault members of the public in unprovoked attacks." If the law supposes that, as Mr. Bumble said in *Oliver Twist*, "the law is a ass—a idiot."

As for Peter Wareing, even in his brain-damaged state, he had a better appreciation of things. He was evidently a man of some spirit: having been a salesman, he decided to study for the law, supported himself at law school by a variety of manual jobs, and qualified at the bar at the age of forty. The extent of his recovery astounded his neurosurgeon, who attributed it to Wareing's determination and "bloody-mindedness." He is avid to get back to work, but the contrast between the nominal eighteen-month sentence for his attackers and his own "life sentence," as he called it, of struggle against disability is not lost on him. "If there were real justice," he said, "they would have gone to prison for life." Could any compassionate person disagree?

Perhaps the final insult is that the state is paying for Wareing to have psychotherapy to suppress his anger. "I have this rage inside me for the people who did this," he said. "I truly hate them." Having failed in its primary duty, the state then treats the rage naturally consequent upon this failure as pathological, in need of therapy. On reading Peter Wareing's story, ordinary, decent citizens will themselves feel a sense of impotent rage, despair, betrayal, and abandonment similar to his. Do we all need psychotherapy?

A second case similarly illustrates the refusal of the British state to take the lives of its citizens seriously. An engineer—Philip Carroll, the father of four—was tinkering with his car outside his home. Four drunken youths sat on a wall on his property, and he asked them to leave. They argued with him, and one of them threw a stone at his car. He chased this youth and caught him, but between twenty and forty more youths loitering drunkenly nearby rallied round, and one fifteen-year-old hit the engineer to the ground, where he too banged his head and received severe brain damage. Unconscious for eighteen days, he needed three operations to survive; and now he too has an impaired memory and might never work again.

According to his parents, the culprit, Michael Kuba-Kuba, felt deeply ashamed of what he had done, but this did not in the least prevent him during the trial from claiming (unsuccessfully, in the event) that he had been acting in self-defense. This does not sound like genuine shame to me but rather an attempt to get away with it. Before passing sentence, the judge said: "I have to try to ensure that the courts will treat incidents like this with great severity, to send out a message to other young people that violence is not acceptable."

Another prelude, you might think, to a stiff sentence—but again you would be wrong. The young man got twelve months, of which he will serve six. Six months for the active life of a man—for having caused thirty or forty years of disability as well as incalculable suffering to the disabled man's family! It is not difficult to imagine Kuba-Kuba returning from prison to a hero's welcome, because he had simultaneously gotten away

with near-murder and survived the rite of passage that imprisonment now represents. The message the judge sent out to other
young people, no doubt unintentionally, was that youths may
destroy other people's lives with virtual impunity, for the British
state does not care in the least about protecting them or deter-
ring such crimes.

Two aspects of the case went unexamined in the newspapers. The first was that Kuba-Kuba's parents were the owners of
a grocery store specializing in African foods, and were deeply
religious. The young man doubtless did not grow up in abject
poverty, then; nor would he have derived his readiness for violence from anything his parents might have taught him.

The second was that Kuba-Kuba was a talented athlete, apparently of Olympic standard. He was a promising soccer
player, so promising that several major teams were seriously interested in recruiting him. If, as seemed likely, he had made the
grade, he would have become a multimillionaire by his early
twenties, earning more in a year than most people in a lifetime.
Lack of economic prospects and the frustration it entails can
hardly explain a propensity to violence in his case, therefore.

We must look elsewhere for the source of his violent conduct. Possibly he was born a sport of nature, a creature biologically destined to violence—no doubt there are such cases. But
far more likely was that an aggressive popular culture that glo-
rifies egotistical impulsivity and denigrates self-control influenced him. Although his parents presented him, in their statements, as a paragon of virtue, he already had a conviction for
theft, and he clearly hung about with teenagers who drank a lot
and made a nuisance of themselves. Carroll confronted the
youth who threw the stone precisely because he was exasperated by the unruly behavior that prevailed in his neighborhood,
undeterred and unpunished by the state. A senior policeman
said after the attack, "We have gangs of young people hanging
around on street corners being abusive, intimidating and caus-

ing trouble. . . . They don't give a damn about the police or the criminal justice system."

And who can blame them? What deterrent, punishment, vengeance, or protection for society is six months in prison for having injured a man so badly that he did not recognize his wife or children for several months afterward, that he now has poor eyesight, has lost his sense of smell and taste, has to wear a brace on one foot and a hard hat to protect his skull, and says of himself, "I just have no interest in anything or anyone"—having previously been a highly successful man?

Having seen how the British state takes the serious lightly, let us now see how it takes the trivial seriously.

The newspapers reported the case of an Oxford student who, slightly drunk after celebrating the end of his exams, approached a mounted policeman. "Excuse me," said the young man to the policeman, "do you realize your horse is gay?"

This was not a very witty remark, but it was hardly filled with deep malice either. It was, perhaps, a manifestation of the youthful silliness of which most of us have been guilty in our time. And Oxford was once a city in which drunken students often played, and were even expected to play, pranks on the police, such as knocking off their helmets.

The policeman did not think the student's remark was innocent, however. He called two squad cars to his aid, and, in a city in which it is notoriously difficult to interest the police in so trivial a matter as robbery or burglary, they arrived almost at once. Apparently, the mounted policeman thought—if thought is quite the word I seek—that the young man's remark was likely to "cause harassment, alarm or distress." He was arrested and charged under the Public Order Act for having made a "homophobic remark."

The young man spent a night in jail. Brought before the magistrates the following day, he was fined $140, which he refused to pay. The police then sent the case to the equivalent of the district attorney, who brought the student before the courts again but had to admit that there was not enough evidence to prove that his conduct had been disorderly.

The degree to which political correctness has addled British consciousness, like a computer virus, and destroyed all our traditional attachment to liberty, is illustrated by the words of one of the student's friends who witnessed the incident. "[His] comments were . . . in jest," he said. "It was very clear that they were not homophobic." In other words, the friend accepted the premise that certain remarks, well short of incitement to commit violence or any actual crime—words that merely expressed an unpopular or intolerant point of view—would have constituted reasonable grounds for arrest. One consequence of the liberal intelligentsia's long march through the institutions is the acceptance of the category of Thoughtcrime. On the other hand, political correctness permits genuine incitement to murder—such as the BEHEAD THOSE WHO INSULT ISLAM placards carried by Muslim demonstrators in London four months after the publication of cartoons of Mohammed in a Danish newspaper—to go completely unpunished. Other people, other customs.

Goodness knows how much time of how many people this episode in Oxford had wasted, and at what cost to the taxpayer—all in a country with the highest rate of crime (that is to say, of real crime) in the Western world. I could not help comparing the alacrity with which the police dealt with the "homophobic" remark with their indifference to an act of arson my wife witnessed shortly before we left England.

She noticed some youths setting fire to the contents of a Dumpster just outside our house, a fire that could easily have spread to cars parked nearby. She called the police.

"What do you expect us to do about it?" they asked.

"I expect you to come and arrest them," she said.

The police regarded this as a bizarre and unreasonable expectation. They refused point-blank to send anyone. Of course, if they had promised to make every effort to come quickly but had arrived too late, or even not at all, my wife would have understood and been satisfied. But she was not satisfied with the idea that youths could set dangerous fires without arousing even the minimal interest of the police. Surely some or all of the youths would conclude that they could do anything they liked, and move on to more serious crimes.

My wife then insisted that the police should at least place the crime on their records. Again they refused. She remonstrated with them at length, and at considerable cost to her equanimity. At last, and with the greatest reluctance, they recorded the crime and gave her a reference number for it.

This was not the end of the matter. About fifteen minutes later a more senior policeman telephoned to upbraid her and tell her she had been wasting police time with her insistence on satisfaction in so trivial a matter. The police, apparently, had more important things to do than suppress arson. Goodness knows what homophobic remarks were being made while the youths were merely setting a fire that could have spread, and in the process learning that they could do so with impunity.

It is not difficult to guess the reason for the senior policeman's anger. My wife had forced his men to record a crime that they had no intention whatever of even trying to solve (though, with due expedition, it was eminently soluble), and this record in turn meant the introduction of an unwanted breath of reality into the bogus statistics, the manufacture of which is now every British senior policeman's principal task—with the sole exception of enforcing the dictates of political correctness, thereby to head off the criticism levied at them for many decades by the liberal left—not always without an element of justification. Proving their purity of heart is now more important to them than securing the safety of our streets: and thus Nero fiddled while Rome burned.

Another story in the newspaper then caught my eye: the government wanted to ban smoking in British prisons.

At first sight this might seem like a serious rather than a frivolous idea. More than nine-tenths of prisoners smoke, and if they continue to do so, about half of them will die prematurely as a result. The evidence that smoking is bad for the health has long since been overwhelming and incontrovertible. Therefore the government could reasonably claim that the proposed ban was evidence of its solicitude for the welfare of the most despised of all sections of society, prisoners. And after all, what could be more serious, less frivolous, than saving lives, or trying to do so?

In general I am not sentimental about the rights of prisoners. I don't think the proposed ban infringes any of their rights; but it seems to me that there are plenty of reasons for treating prisoners decently and humanely other than the observance of their supposed rights. Decency and humanity are goods in themselves, after all. The proposed ban was not only hypocritical but gratuitously cruel and inhumane, and likely to prove ineffective into the bargain.

But it would be wrong even if effective.

Smoking is not illegal in Britain, and the government derives large revenues from the consumption of tobacco, indeed far larger than the profits of the tobacco companies. It uses these revenues not to lessen the taxes of nonsmokers but merely as one among many other sources of revenue. Although high taxation on tobacco does discourage smoking, that is not, and never was, its primary aim.

At bottom the proposal looks like the arbitrary bullying of a defenseless population in a fit of Pecksniffian moral enthusiasm. It is to deprive that population of a small privilege long accepted by custom and usage. And, of course, the moral enthusiasts of the government will not bear the practical cost of enforcing the ban; the prison wardens will. The proposal is an example of the soft and creeping totalitarianism that comes with unctuous offers of benefits and avowals of purity of intention, rather than the boot-in-the-face variety of Orwell's description. It is the insinuation of the government into the nooks and crannies of everyday life, on the pretext that people are incapable of deciding anything for themselves. Everyone is a child for whom the government is in permanent loco parentis (except children, of course, who can consent to sex at age sixteen and are to be given the vote at the same age, if Chancellor Brown has his way).

The newspapers confirmed what I had long perceived before I left Britain: that the zeitgeist of the country is now one of sentimental moralizing combined with the utmost cynicism, where the government's pretended concern for the public welfare coexists with the most elementary dereliction of duty. There is an absence of any kind of idealism that is a necessary precondition of probity, so that bad faith prevails almost everywhere. The government sees itself as an engineer of souls (to use the phrase so eloquently coined by Stalin with regard to writers who, of course, were expected to mold Homo Sovieticus by the power of their words). Government thus concerns itself with what people think, feel, and say—as well as with trying to change their freely chosen habits—rather than with performing its one inescapable duty: that of preserving the peace and ensuring that citizens may go about their lawful business in confidence and safety. It is more concerned that young men should not smoke cigarettes in prison or make silly jokes to policemen than that they should not attack and permanently maim their elders and betters.

One definition of decadence is the concentration on the gratifyingly imaginary to the disregard of the disconcertingly real. No one who knows Britain could doubt that it has very serious problems—economic, social, and cultural. Its public services— which already consume a vast proportion of the national wealth—are not only inefficient but completely beyond amelioration by the expenditure of yet more money. Its population is abysmally educated, to the extent that in a few more years Britain will not even have a well-educated elite. An often cynical and criminally minded population has been indoctrinated with shallow and gimcrack notions—for example, about social justice—that render it singularly unfit to compete in an increasingly competitive world. Not coincidentally, Britain has serious economic problems, even if the government has managed so far—in the eyes of the world, at least—to paper over the cracks. Unpleasant realities cannot be indefinitely disguised or conjured away, however.

Therefore I have removed myself: not that I imagine things are much better, only slightly different, in France. But one does not feel the defects of a foreign country in quite the same lacerating way as the defects of one's native land; they are more an object of amused, detached interest than of personal despair.

2006

Real Crime, Fake Justice

◈ FOR THE LAST FORTY YEARS, government policy in Britain, de facto if not always de jure, has been to render the British population virtually defenseless against criminals and criminality. Almost alone of British government policies, this one has been supremely effective: no Briton nowadays goes many hours without wondering how to avoid being victimized by a criminal intent on theft, burglary, or violence.

An unholy alliance between politicians and bureaucrats who want to keep prison costs to a minimum, and liberal intellectuals who pretend to see in crime a natural and understandable response to social injustice—which it would be a further injustice to punish—has engendered a prolonged and so far unfinished experiment in leniency that has debased the quality of life of millions of people, especially the poor. Every day in our newspapers we read of the absurd and dangerous leniency of the criminal-justice system. On April 21, for example, even the *Observer* (one of the bastions of British liberalism responsible for the present situation) gave prominence to the official report into the case of Anthony Rice, who strangled and then stabbed Naomi Bryant to death.

Rice, it turned out, had been assaulting women since 1972. He had been convicted for assaulting or raping a total of fifteen women before murdering Naomi Bryant, and it is a fair supposition that he had assaulted or raped many more who did not go to the police. In 1982 he grabbed a woman by the throat, held a knife to her, and raped her. Five years later, while out of prison on home leave, he grabbed a woman, pushed her into a garden, held a knife to her, and raped her for an hour. Receiving a life sentence, he was transferred to an open prison in 2002 and then released two years later on parole as a low-risk parolee. He received housing in a hostel for ex-prisoners in a village whose inhabitants had been told, to gain their acquiescence, that none of the residents there was violent; five months after his arrival, he murdered Naomi Bryant. In pronouncing another life sentence on him, the judge ordered that he should serve at least twenty-five years: in other words, even now the law has not quite thrown away the key.

Only five days later the papers reported that 1,023 prisoners of foreign origin had been released from British prisons between 1999 and 2006 without having been deported. Among them were five killers, seven kidnappers, nine rapists, and 39 other sex offenders, four arsonists, 41 burglars, 52 thieves, 93 robbers, and 204 drug offenders. Of the 1,023 prisoners, only 106 had since been traced. The Home Office, responsible for both prisons and immigration, still doesn't know how many of the killers, arsonists, rapists, and kidnappers are at large; but it admits that most of them will never be found, at least until they are caught after committing another offense. Although these revelations forced the home secretary to resign, in fact the foreign criminals had been treated only as British criminals are treated. At least we can truly say that we do not discriminate in our leniency.

Scandal has followed scandal. A short time later we learned that prisoners had been absconding from one open prison, Leyhill, at a rate of two a week for three years—323 in total since 1999, among them 22 murderers. This outrage came to light only when a senior policeman in the area of Leyhill told a member of Parliament that there had been a crime wave in the vicinity of the prison. The member of Parliament demanded the figures in the House of Commons; otherwise they would have remained secret.

None of these revelations, however, would have surprised a man called David Fraser, who has just published a book entitled *A Land Fit for Criminals*—the land in question being Great Britain, of course. Far from being mistakes—for mistakes repeated so often cease to be mere mistakes—all these occurrences are in full compliance with general policy in Britain with regard to crime and criminality.

Fraser was a probation officer for more than a quarter of a century. He began to doubt the value of his work in terms of preventing crime and therefore protecting the public, but at first he assumed that, as a comparatively lowly official in the criminal-justice system, he was too mired in the grainy everyday detail to see the bigger picture. He assumed also that those in charge not only knew what they were doing but had the public interest at heart.

Eventually, however, the penny dropped. Fraser's lack of success in effecting any change in the criminals under his supervision, and thus in reducing the number of crimes that they subsequently committed, to the great misery of the general public, was not his failure alone but was general throughout the system. Even worse, he discovered that the bureaucrats who ran the system, and their political masters, did not care about this failure, at least from the point of view of its impact on public safety; careerist to the core, they were concerned only that the public should not become aware of the catastrophe. To this end they indulged in obfuscation, statistical legerdemain, and outright lies in order to prevent the calamity that public knowledge of the truth would represent for them and their careers.

The collective intellectual dishonesty of those who worked in the system so outraged Fraser—and the Kafkaesque world in which he found himself, where nothing was called by its real

name and language tended more to conceal meaning than to
convey it, so exasperated him—that, though not a man apt to
obtrude upon the public, he determined to write a book. It took
him two and a half years to do so, based on twenty years of research, and it is clear from the very first page that he wrote it
from a burning need to expose and exorcise the lies and evasions with which he lived for so long, lies and evasions that
helped in a few decades transform a law-abiding country with a
reputation for civility into the country with the highest crime
rate in the Western world, with an ever-present undercurrent of
violence in daily life. Like Luther, Fraser could not but speak
out. And, as events unfolded, his book has had a publishing history that is additionally revealing of the state of Britain today.

By example after example (repetition being necessary to establish that he has not just alighted on an isolated case of absurdity that might be found in any large-scale enterprise), Fraser
demonstrates the unscrupulous lengths to which both bureaucrats and governments have gone to disguise from the public the
effect of their policies and decisions, carried out with an almost
sadistic indifference to the welfare of common people.

He shows that liberal intellectuals and their bureaucratic
allies have left no stone unturned to ensure that the law-abiding should be left as defenseless as possible against the preda-
tions of criminals, from the emasculation of the police to the
devising of punishments that do not punish and the propagation of sophistry by experts to mislead and confuse the public
about what is happening in society, confusion rendering the
public helpless in the face of the experimentation perpetrated
upon it.

The police, Fraser shows, are like a nearly defeated occupy-
ing colonial force that, while mayhem reigns everywhere else,
has retreated to safe enclaves, there to shuffle paper and produce bogus information to propitiate its political masters. Their
first line of defense is to refuse to record half the crime that

comes to their attention, which itself is less than half the crime committed. Then they refuse to investigate recorded crime, or to arrest the culprits even when it is easy to do so and the evidence against them is overwhelming, because the prosecuting author-ities will either decline to prosecute, or else the resultant sen-tence will be so trivial as to make the whole procedure (at least nineteen forms to fill in after a single arrest) pointless.

In any case, the authorities want the police to use a sanction known as the caution—a mere verbal warning. Indeed, as Fraser points out, the Home Office even reprimanded the West Mid-lands Police Force for bringing too many apprehended offend-ers to court, instead of merely giving them a caution. In the of-ficial version, only minor crimes are dealt with in this fashion: but as Fraser points out, in the year 2000 alone, 600 cases of robbery, 4,300 cases of car theft, 6,600 offenses of burglary, 13,400 offenses against public order, 35,400 cases of violence against the person, and 67,600 cases of other kinds of theft were dealt with in this fashion—in effect, letting these 127,900 offenders off scot-free. When one considers that the police clear-up rate of all crimes in Britain is scarcely more than one in 20 (and even that figure is based upon official deception), the lib-eral intellectual claim, repeated ad nauseam in the press and on the air, that the British criminal-justice system is primitively retributive is absurd.

At every point in the system, Fraser shows, deception reigns. When a judge sentences a criminal to three years' imprisonment, he knows perfectly well (as does the press that reports it) that in the vast majority of cases the criminal in question will serve eighteen months at the very most, because he is entitled auto-matically, as of right, to a suspension of half his sentence. More-over, under a scheme of early release, increasingly used, prison-ers serve considerably less than half their sentence. They may be tagged electronically under a system of home curfew, intended to give the public an assurance that they are being monitored:

but the electronic tag stays on for fewer than twelve hours daily, giving criminals plenty of opportunity to follow their careers. Even when the criminals remove their tags (and it is known that thousands are removed or vandalized every year) or fail to abide by other conditions of their early release, those who are supposedly monitoring them do nothing whatever, for fear of spoiling the statistics of the system's success. When the Home Office tried the tagging system with young criminals, 73 percent of them were reconvicted within three months. The authorities nevertheless decided to extend the scheme. The failure of the British state to take its responsibilities seriously could not be more clearly expressed.

Fraser draws attention to the deeply corrupt system in Britain under which a criminal, once caught, may ask for other offenses that he has committed to be "taken into consideration." (Criminals call these offenses TICs.) This practice may be in the interests of both the criminal and the police, but not in those of the long-suffering public. The court will sentence the criminal to further prison terms that run concurrently, not consecutively, to that imposed for the index offense: in other words, he will in effect serve the same sentence for fifty burglaries as for one burglary, and he can never again face charges for the forty-nine burglaries that have been "taken into consideration." Meanwhile the police can preen themselves that they have "solved" fifty crimes for the price of one.

One Probation Service smokescreen that Fraser knows from personal experience is to measure its own effectiveness by the proportion of criminals who complete their probation in compliance with court orders—a procedural outcome that has no significance whatever for the safety of the public. Such criminals come under the direct observation of probation officers only one hour a week at the very most. What they do the other 167 hours of the week the probation officers cannot possibly know. Unless one takes the preposterous view that such criminals are incapable of telling lies about their activities to their probation officers, mere attendance at the probation office is no guarantee whatever that they are now leading law-abiding lives.

But even if completion of probation orders were accepted as a surrogate measure of success in preventing reoffending, the Probation Service's figures have long been completely corrupt—and for a very obvious reason. Until 1997 the probation officers themselves decided when noncompliance with their directions was so egregious that they "breached" the criminals under their supervision and returned them to the courts because of such noncompliance. Since their own effectiveness was measured by the proportion of probation orders "successfully" completed, they had a very powerful motive for disregarding the noncompliance of criminals. In such circumstances all activity became strictly pro forma, with no purpose external to itself.

While the government put an end to this particular statistical legerdemain, probation orders still go into the statistics as "successfully completed" if they reach their official termination date—even in many cases if the offender gets arrested for committing further offenses before that date. Only in this way can the Home Office claim that between 70 and 80 percent of probation orders are "successfully completed."

In their effort to prove the liberal orthodoxy that prison does not work, criminologists, government officials, and journalists have routinely used the lower reconviction rates of those sentenced to probation and other forms of noncustodial punishment (the word "punishment" in these circumstances being used very loosely) than those imprisoned. But if the aim is to protect the law-abiding, a comparison of reconviction rates of those imprisoned and those put on probation is irrelevant. What counts is the reoffending rate—a point so obvious that it is shameful that Fraser should not only have to make it but to hammer it home repeatedly, for the politicians, academics, and journalistic hangers-on have completely obscured it.

By definition, a man in prison can commit no crimes (except against fellow prisoners and prison staff). But what of those out in the world on probation? Of 1,000 male criminals on probation, Fraser makes clear, about 600 will be reconvicted at least once within the two years that the Home Office follows them up for statistical purposes. The rate of detection in Britain of all crimes being about 5 percent, those 1,000 criminals will actually have committed not 600, but at least 12,000 crimes (assuming them to have been averagely competent criminals chased by averagely incompetent police). Even this is not quite all. Since there are, in fact, about 150,000 people on probation in Britain, it means that at least 1.8 million crimes—more than an eighth of the nation's total—must be committed annually by people on probation, within the very purview of the criminal-justice system, or very shortly after they have been on probation. While some of these crimes might be "victimless," or at least impersonal, research has shown that these criminals inflict untold misery upon the British population: misery that they would not have been able to inflict had they been in prison for a year instead of on probation.

To compare the reconviction rates of ex-prisoners and people on probation as an argument against prison is not only irrelevant from the point of view of public safety but is also logically absurd. *Of course* the imprisoned will have higher reconviction rates once they get out of jail—not because prison failed to reform them but because it is the most hardened, incorrigible, and recidivist criminals who go to prison. Again, this point is so obvious that it is shameful that anyone should have to point it out; yet politicians and others continue to use the reconviction rates as if they were a proper basis for deciding policy.

Relentless for hundreds of pages, Fraser provides examples of how the British government and its bloated and totally ineffectual bureaucratic apparatus, through moral and intellectual frivolity as well as plain incompetence, has failed in its elementary and sole inescapable duty: to protect the lives and property of the citizenry. He exposes the absurd prejudice that has become a virtually unassailable orthodoxy among the intellectual and political elite: that we have too many prisoners in Britain, as if there were an ideal number of prisoners, derived from a purely abstract principle, at which, independent of the number of crimes committed, we should aim. He describes in full detail the moral and intellectual corruption of the British criminal-justice system, from police decisions not to record crimes or to charge wrongdoers, to the absurdly light sentences given after conviction and the administrative means by which prisoners end up serving less than half their time, irrespective of their dangerousness or the likelihood that they will reoffend.

According to Fraser, at the heart of the British idiocy is the condescending and totally unrealistic idea—which, however, provides employment opportunities for armies of apparatchiks as well as being psychologically gratifying—that burglars, thieves, and robbers are not conscious malefactors who calculate their chances of getting away with it, but people in the grip of something rather like a mental disease, whose thoughts, feelings, and decision-making processes need to be restructured. The whole criminal-justice system ought therefore to act in a therapeutic or medical, rather than a punitive and deterrent, fashion. Burglars do not know, poor things, that householders are upset by housebreaking, and so we must educate and inform them on this point; and we must also seek to persuade them of something that all their experience so far has taught them to be false, namely that crime does not pay.

All in all, Fraser's book is a searing and unanswerable (or at least so far unanswered) indictment of the British criminal-justice system, and therefore of the British state. As Fraser pointed out to me, the failure of the state to protect the lives and property of its citizens, and to take seriously its duty in this regard, creates a politically dangerous situation, for it puts the very legitimacy of

the state itself at risk. The potential consequences are incalculable, for the failure might bring the rule of law itself into disrepute
and give an opportunity to the brutal and the authoritarian.

You might have thought that any publisher would gratefully
accept a book so urgent in its message, so transparently the
product of a burning need to communicate obvious but uncomfortable truths of such public interest, conveyed in such a way
that anyone of reasonable intelligence might understand them.
Any publisher, you would think, would feel fortunate to have
such a manuscript land on his desk. But you would be wrong,
at least as far as Britain is concerned.

So uncongenial was Fraser's message to all right-thinking
Britons that sixty publishers to whom he sent the book turned
it down. In a country that publishes more than ten thousand
books monthly, not many of which are imperishable master-
pieces, there was no room for it or for what it said, though it
would take no great acumen to see its commercial possibilities
in a country crowded with crime victims. So great was the pressure of the orthodoxy now weighing on the minds of the British
intelligentsia that Fraser might as well have gone to Mecca and
said that there is no God and that Mohammed was not His
prophet. Of course, no publisher actually told him that what he
said was unacceptable or unsayable in public: his book merely
did not "fit the list" of any publisher. He was the victim of
British publishing's equivalent of Mafia *omerta*.

Fortunately he did not give up, as he sometimes thought of
doing. The sixty-first publisher to whom he sent the book accepted it. I mean no disrespect to her judgment when I say that
it was her personal situation that distinguished her from her fellow publishers: for her husband's son by a previous marriage
had not long before been murdered in the street, stabbed by a
drug-dealing Jamaican immigrant, aged twenty, who had not
been deported despite his criminal record but instead allowed to
stay in the country as if he were a national treasure to be at all

costs cherished and nurtured. Indeed, in court his lawyer presented him as an unemployed painter and decorator, the victim of racial prejudice (a mitigating circumstance, of course), a view that the prosecution did not challenge, even though the killer had somehow managed alchemically to transmute his unemployment benefits into a new convertible costing some $54,000.

The maternal grandmother of the murdered boy, who had never been ill in her life, died of a heart attack a week after his death, and so the funeral was a double one. It is difficult to resist the conclusion that the killer killed not one but two people. He received a sentence of eight years—which, in effect, will be four or five years.

I asked the publisher the impossible question of whether she would have published the book if someone close to her had not had such firsthand experience of the frivolous leniency of the British criminal-justice system. She said she thought so: but what is beyond dispute is that the murder made her publication of the book a certainty.

A Land Fit for Criminals has sold well and has been very widely discussed, though not by the most important liberal newspapers, which would find the whole subject in bad taste. But the book's publishing history demonstrates how close we have come to an almost totalitarian uniformity of the sayable, imposed informally by right-thinking people in the name of humanity, but in utter disregard for the truth and the reality of their fellow citizens' lives. Better that they, the right-thinking, should feel pleased with their own rectitude and broadmindedness, than that millions should be freed of their fear of robbery and violence. Too bad Fraser's voice had to be heard over someone's dead body.

2006

Delusions of Honesty

WHEN TONY BLAIR announced his resignation after ten years as prime minister of the United Kingdom, his voice choked with emotion and he nearly shed a tear. He asked his audience to believe that he had always done what he thought was right. He would have been nearer the mark had he said that he always thought that what was right was whatever he had done. Throughout his years in office, he kept inviolable his belief in the existence of a purely beneficent essence of himself, a belief so strong that no quantity of untruthfulness, shady dealings, unscrupulousness, or constitutional impropriety could undermine or destroy it. Having come into the world marked by Original Virtue, Blair was also a natural-born preacher.

In a confessional mood, Blair admitted that he had sometimes fallen short of what was expected of him. He did not give specifics, but we were expected to admire his candor and humility in making such an admission. It is no coincidence, however, that Blair reached maturity at the time of the publication of the famous book *Psychobabble*, which dissects the modern tendency to indulge in self-obsession without self-examination. Here was a *mea culpa* without the *culpa*. Bless me, people (Blair appeared to be saying), for I have sinned: but please don't ask me to say how.

There undoubtedly were things to be grateful for during the Blair years. His support for American policy in Iraq won him much sympathy in the United States, of course. He was often eloquent in defense of liberty. And under Blair's leadership, Britain enjoyed ten years of uninterrupted economic growth, leaving large parts of the country prosperous as never before. London became one of the world's richest cities, vying with New York to be the global economy's financial center. Blair did inherit a strapping economy from his predecessor, and he left its management more or less to the man who succeeds him, Gordon Brown. Still, unlike previous Labour prime ministers, he did not preside over an economic crisis: in itself, something to be proud of.

But how history will judge him overall, and whether it will absolve him (to adapt slightly a phrase coined by a famous, though now ailing, Antillean dictator), is another matter. Strictly speaking, history doesn't absolve, or for that matter vindicate, anybody; only people absolve or vindicate, and except in the most obvious cases of villainy or sainthood, they come to different conclusions, using basically the same evidence. There can thus be no definitive judgment of Blair, especially one contemporaneous with his departure. Still, I will try.

Blair's resignation announcement was typical of the man and, one must admit, of the new culture from which he emerged: lachrymose and self-serving. It revealed an unfailing eye and ear for the ersatz and the kitsch, which allowed him so long to play upon the sensibilities of a large section of the population as upon a pipe.

He knew exactly what to say of Princess Diana when she died in a car accident, for example: that she was "the people's princess." He sensed acutely that the times were not so much democratic as demotic: that economic egalitarianism having suffered a decisive defeat both in theory and practice, the only mass appeal left to a politician calling himself radical was to cultural egalitarianism. He could gauge the feelings of the people because, in large part, he shared them. A devotee himself of the cult of celebrity, in which the marriage of glamour and banality both reassures democratic sentiment and stimulates fantasies of luxury, he sought the company of minor show-business personalities and stayed in their homes during his holidays. The practical demonstration that he worshipped at the same shrines as the people did, that his tastes were the same as theirs, more than compensated for the faint odor of impropriety that this gave off. And differences of taste, after all, unite or divide men more profoundly than anything else.

No prime minister had ever been at once so ubiquitous and so inaccessible. Instinctively understanding the dynamics of the cult of celebrity, Blair was both familiar (he insisted on being known by a diminutive) and distant (he acted more as head of state than as head of government, and spent three times more on his own office than did his predecessor). Having invited sixty ordinary citizens into Downing Street so that they could give him their views, and so that he could say he listened to the people, he proceeded to address them via a huge plasma screen, though he was in the building. So near, and yet so far: this was a grand vizier's durbar for the age of virtual reality. With Blair, communication, like time's arrow, flew in one direction only.

Tony Blair was the perfect politician for an age of short attention spans. What he said on one day had no necessary connection with what he said on the following day: and if someone pointed out the contradiction, he would use his favorite phrase, "It's time to move on," as if detecting contradictions in what he said were some kind of curious psychological symptom in the person detecting them.

Many have surmised that there was an essential flaw in Blair's makeup that turned him gradually from the most popular to the most unpopular prime minister of recent history. The problem is to name that essential flaw. As a psychiatrist, I found this problem peculiarly irritating (bearing in mind that it is always highly speculative to make a diagnosis at a distance). But finally a possible solution arrived in a flash of illumination. Blair suffered from a condition previously unknown to me: delusions of honesty.

Blair came to power promising that his government would be "purer than pure," an expression both self-righteous and somewhat foolish, given the fallen nature of man. The Tories preceding him in government had become notorious for acts of corruption that now appear trifling. Indeed, one objection to those acts—for example, asking questions in the House of Commons in return for payment, handed under the table in used banknotes wrapped in brown paper envelopes—was the derisory sums involved. What kind of person would risk ruin for amounts of money that honest people could make in a week or two?

Soon after Blair took office, however, a billionaire named Bernie Ecclestone offered the Labour party a $2 million donation if the government exempted Formula 1 motor racing, which he controlled, from the ban on cigarette ads at sporting events. The government granted the exemption. After public exposure, Blair declared himself to be such a "straight kind of guy" that it was inconceivable that he had involved himself in such an unsavory arrangement—though clearly he had. It was his capacity to believe his own untruths that proved so persuasive to others; it was among his greatest political assets.

Such scandals—involving favors granted to rich men, followed, after exposure, by protestations of injured innocence—punctuated Blair's tenure with monotonous regularity. One of the more notorious was the letter that Blair sent to the Romanian prime minister, Adrian Nastase, encouraging him to sell the state-owned steel producer Sidex to billionaire industrialist Lakshmi Mittal; it would help Romania's application to join the European Union, Blair argued, if a British company bought the steel producer. But Mittal's company was not British; of its 125,000 employees, only 100 worked in Britain; indeed, Mittal himself was not British. He had, however, donated $250,000 to Labour shortly beforehand.

Far from being purer than pure, Blair was laxly forgiving of impropriety in others, provided they were loyal or politically useful to him. The case of Peter Mandelson is particularly instructive. When first a minister, Mandelson borrowed a large sum of money from another minister, Geoffrey Robinson, a multimillionaire, in order to buy a house. Not only did Mandelson fail to tell the bank that lent him the rest of the money for the purchase that the money he had in hand was not his own (in less well-connected mortals, that would be considered fraud); the government department that Mandelson headed at the time was investigating Robinson's own business affairs for suspected improprieties.

Public exposure forced Blair to accept Mandelson's resignation. But the prime minister soon reappointed Mandelson to the cabinet. Blair accepted Mandelson's resignation a second time, however, when it emerged that he had pushed through the passport application of one of the Hinduja brothers, Indian businessmen accused of corruption in India, after a $2 million donation to Labour. Blair then rewarded Mandelson with the lucrative and powerful post of European commissioner. What is one to conclude from this?

Having come into power deeply critical of the previous government's use of private consultants, Blair promptly increased spending on them at least tenfold, ensuring the loyalty of senior civil servants (traditionally a professional cadre, not political appointees) by allowing them to cross back and forth between public and private employment, enriching themselves enormously at public expense in the process. Thus Blair played Mephistopheles to the civil service's Faust, introducing levels of corruption and patronage not seen in Britain since the eighteenth century. Huge sums of money have disappeared, as if into a black hole, into such organizations as the National Health

Service, where bureaucracies have hugely expanded and entwined their interests so closely with those of private suppliers and consultancies that it is difficult to distinguish public from private any longer. Spending on the NHS has increased by two and a half times in the space of ten years; yet it is hard to see any corresponding improvement in the service, other than in the standard of living of those who work in it.

Blair even became the first serving prime minister in history to find himself questioned by the police in Downing Street, under caution of self-incrimination, in the course of a criminal investigation—in this case, into the selling of seats in the House of Lords. Small wonder that for much of the population, truth and Blair now appear to inhabit parallel universes. Reflecting the country's mood is the famous remark that Gordon Brown made to Blair: "There is nothing that you could say to me now that I could ever believe."

Blair proved unusually expert in the postmodernist art of spin. A political adviser to the government perfectly captured this approach on September 11, 2001, when she said that it was "a good day to bury bad news." In other words, you can get away with anything if the timing is right.

At the outset of his tenure, Blair said that his government would be tough on crime and on the causes of crime. He wanted to appeal—and succeeded in appealing—to two constituencies at once: those who wanted criminals locked up, and those who saw crime as the natural consequence of social injustice, a kind of inchoate protest against the conditions in which they lived.

Blair's resultant task was to obfuscate, so that the electorate and even experts could not find out, without great difficulty, what was going on. For example, Blair's government, aware of public unrest about the number of criminals leaving prison only to commit further serious crimes, introduced indeterminate sentencing—open-ended imprisonment—apparently a tough response to repeat offenders. But the reality was different: the sentencing judges still had the discretion to determine such criminals' parole dates, which in England are de facto release dates. The sentences that criminals would serve, in other words, would be no longer than before the new law.

Another way to confuse the public was to corrupt official statistics. In 2006, to take one example, the government dropped three simple but key measures from the compendious statistics that it gathers about people serving community sentences—that is, various kinds of service and supervision outside prison: their criminal histories prior to sentencing, their reconviction rates, and the number given prison sentences while serving their community sentences. Instead it introduced an utterly meaningless measure, at least from a public-safety perspective: the proportion of people with community sentences who abide by such conditions as weekly attendance for an hour at a probation office.

The police also received encouragement to keep crime numbers down by not recording crimes. The crime rate has fallen in part because shoplifting has ceased to be a crime, for instance. Police now deal with it the way they do with parking violations: shoplifters get on-the-spot fines worth half, on average, of the value of the goods they have stolen.

The problem of unemployment in Britain illustrates perfectly the methods that Blair's government used to obscure the truth. The world generally believes that, thanks to Labour's prudent policies, Britain now enjoys low unemployment; indeed, Blair has often lectured other leaders on the subject. The low rate is not strictly a lie: those counted officially as unemployed are today relatively few.

Unfortunately those counted as sick are many; and if you add the numbers of unemployed and sick together, the figure remains remarkably constant in recent years, oscillating around 3.5 million, though the proportion of sick to unemployed has risen rapidly. Approximately 2.7 million people are receiving disability benefits in Britain, 8 or 9 percent of the workforce, highly concentrated in the areas of former unemployment; more people are claiming that psychiatric disorders prevent them from working than are claiming that work is unavailable. In the former coal-mining town of Merthyr Tydfil, about a quarter of the adult population is on disability. Britain is thus the sick man of Europe, though all objective indicators suggest that people are living longer and healthier lives than ever.

Three groups profit from this statistical legerdemain: first, the unemployed themselves, because disability benefits are about 60 percent higher than unemployment benefits, and, once one is receiving them, one does not have to pretend to be looking for work; second, the doctors who make the bogus diagnoses, because by doing so they remove a possible cause of conflict with their patients and, given the assault rate on British doctors, this is important to them; and finally the government, which can claim to have reduced unemployment.

But such obfuscation is destructive of human personality. The unemployed have to pretend something untrue—namely, that they are sick; the medical profession winds up humiliated and dispirited by taking part in fraud; and the government avoids, for a time, real economic problems. Thus the whole of society finds itself corrupted and infantilized by its inability to talk straight; and that Blair could speak with conviction of the low unemployment rate, and believe that he was telling the truth, is to me worse than if he had been a dastardly cynic.

Tony Blair's most alarming characteristic, however, has been his enmity to freedom in his own country, whatever his feelings about it in other countries. No British prime minister in two hundred years has done more to curtail civil liberties than has Blair. Starting with an assumption of his infinite beneficence, he assumed infinite responsibility, with the result that Britain has become a country with a degree of official surveillance that would make a Latin American military dictator envious. Sometimes this surveillance is merely ludicrous—parking-enforcement officers wearing miniature closed-circuit security cameras in their caps to capture abusive responses from those ticketed, say, or local councils attaching sensing devices to the garbage cans of three million homes to record what people throw away, in order to charge them for the quantity and quality of their trash.

But often the government's reach is less innocuous. For example, in the name of national security the government under Blair's leadership sought to make passport applicants provide two hundred pieces of information about themselves, including bank-account details, and undergo interrogation for half an hour. If an applicant refused to allow the information to circulate through other government departments, he would not receive a passport, with no appeal. The government also cooked up a plan to require passport holders to inform the police if they changed their address.

A justification presented for these Orwellian arrangements was the revelation that a would-be terrorist, Dhiren Barot, had managed to obtain nine British passports before his arrest because he did not want an accumulation of stamps from suspect countries in any of them. At the same time it came to light that the Passport Office issues ten thousand passports a year to fraudulent applicants—hardly surprising since its staff consists largely of immigrants, legal and illegal.

As was often the case with Blair and his government, the solution proposed was not only completely disproportionate to the problem, it was not even a solution. The government has admitted that criminal gangs have already forged the UK's new high-tech passports. The only people, then, whom the process will trouble are the people who need no surveillance. No sensible person denies the danger of Islamic extremism in Britain; but just as the fact that the typical Briton finds himself recorded by security cameras three hundred times a day does not secure him in the slightest from crime or anti-social behavior, which remain prevalent in Britain, so no one feels any safer from the terrorist threat despite the ever-increasing government surveillance.

Blair similarly showed no respect for precedent and gradual reform by Parliament itself, which—in the absence of an American-style written constitution—have been the nation's guiding principles. By decree he made the civil service answerable to unelected political allies for the first time in history; he devoted far less attention to Parliament than did any previous prime minister; the vast majority of legislation under his premiership (amounting to a blizzard so great that lawyers cannot keep up with it) passed without effective parliamentary oversight, in effect by decree; one new criminal offense was created every day except Sundays for ten years, 60 percent of them by such decree, ranging from the selling of grey squirrels and Japanese bindweed to failure to nominate someone to turn off your house alarm if it triggers while you are out; he abolished the independence of the House of Lords, the only and very limited restraint on the elected government's power; he eliminated the immemorial jurisprudential rule against double jeopardy; he wanted to introduce preventive detention for people whom doctors deemed dangerous, even though they had as yet committed no crime; he passed a Civil Contingencies Act that permits the British government, if it believes that an emergency anywhere in the world threatens serious damage to human welfare or to the environment in Britain, to confiscate or destroy property without compensation.

That Blair should have turned out to be so authoritarian ought to come as no surprise to those who listened to the timbre of some of his early pronouncements. His early emphasis on youth; his pursuit of what he called, grandiosely, the Third Way (as if no one had thought of it before); his desire to create a "New Britain"; his assertion that the Labour party was the political arm of the British people (as if people who did not support it were in some way not British)—some have thought all this contained a Mussolinian, or possibly Peronist, ring. It is ridiculous to say that Tony Blair was a fascist; but it would be equally absurd to see him as a defender of liberty, at least in his own country.

Blair found the Muslim threat far easier to tackle abroad than at home, perhaps because it required less courage. Intentionally or not, he pandered to domestic Muslim sentiment. During the general election, in which the leader and deputy leader of the opposition were Jewish, he allowed Labour to portray them as pigs on election campaign posters. The Jewish vote in Britain is small, and scattered throughout the country; the Muslim vote is large, and concentrated in constituencies upon which the whole election might turn. It is not that Blair is anti-Semitic: no one would accuse him of that. It is simply that, if mildly anti-Semitic connotations served his purposes, he would use them, doubtless convinced that it was for the higher good of mankind.

Further, Blair's wife, Cherie, is a lawyer who now practices little but who by convenient coincidence—immediately before a general election, and at a time of Muslim disaffection with Labour over the Iraq War—appeared before the highest court in the land, defending a fifteen-year-old girl who claimed the right to wear full Muslim dress in school. It turned out that an extreme British Islamic group backed the case legally and financially.

Blair also presided over the extension of mail voting in Muslim areas, despite having been warned about the likely consequence: that frequently the male heads of households would vote for all registered voters under their roofs. Indeed, it is difficult to resist the conclusion that Blair supported voting by mail because of this consequence, which would tip the vote toward the many Labour candidates who were Muslim men themselves. Pro-Labour fraud became so widespread that the judge leading a judicial inquiry into an election in Birmingham concluded that it would have disgraced a banana republic. The prime minister also proved exceptionally feeble during the Danish cartoon crisis, and repeatedly said things about Islam—that it is a religion of peace, for one—that he must have known to be untrue.

Blair, then, is no hero. Many in Britain believe that he has been the worst prime minister in recent British history, morally and possibly financially corrupt, shallow and egotistical, a man who combined the qualities of Elmer Gantry with those of Juan Domingo Perón. America should think twice about taking him to its heart now that he has stepped down.

2007

The Terrorists Among Us

◆ WHILE I WAS on a visit to Toronto recently, police arrested seventeen men, the oldest of them forty-three but most much younger, on charges of plotting a terrorist attack. They wished, apparently, to blow up the Parliament in Ottawa and publicly behead the prime minister. Cops caught them in the process of buying three times as much material for explosives as Timothy McVeigh used in the Oklahoma City bombing. Reporting the arrests, the *New York Times* called the men "South Asians"—though one of them was an Egyptian, two were Somali, and most had been born in Canada—thus concealing by an inaccurate euphemism the most salient characteristic of the alleged plotters: they were all Muslims. The Canadian police, emasculated and even stupefied by the exigencies of political correctness (the modern bellwether of virtue), said that the seventeen came from such diverse backgrounds that they were unable to discern anything in common among them.

Canadians, on the whole, reacted to news of the plot with a mixture of outrage and disbelief. A few responded more vigorously, smashing the windows of a Toronto mosque, which the press swiftly denounced as un-Canadian. But many wondered, why us? when Canada had been among the most tolerant and accommodating countries to its immigrants in the world, and where celebration of diversity for its own sake had been made almost an official fetish. Could it be that no liberal policy goes unpunished?

It rapidly became clear that no single sociological factor of the kind usually invoked to explain outrageous behavior—poverty, say, or racial discrimination—could explain the adherence of all seventeen to the plot (assuming that the charges against them are true). The Somalis involved were born in Somalia in the midst of the chronic civil war there and came to Canada as refugees, where they soon fell into unideological delinquency before catching the Islamist bug; they were not economic success stories. Other alleged plotters, however, emerged from the well-integrated middle classes, such as the son of a successful doctor of Indian origin who had emigrated to Canada from Trinidad. The pictures of the houses in which some of the plotters lived and grew up must have made more than a few newspaper readers envious. Whatever explained the resort of the seventeen to the scimitar and the bomb, raw poverty or the hopelessness of insuperable discrimination was not it.

It so happened that the Toronto arrests coincided with the publication in America of a novel by the distinguished writer John Updike, called *Terrorist*. This novel is an attempt to enter the mental world not of a young Canadian but of a young American would-be Islamist bomber. It received, to put it mildly, mixed reviews emphasizing its weaknesses far more than its strengths. Sociological or psychological accuracy and acuteness cannot entirely compensate for literary shortcomings in what is, after all, a literary artifact, but in view of the importance of the subject and the dearth of other attempts to treat it imaginatively, I think Updike deserves more credit than he has received.

The story concerns a young man called Ahmad Ashmawy Mulloy, the son of an Irish-American mother and an Egyptian immigrant father. The mother is a nurse's aide in a hospital and an aspiring, though untalented, amateur artist. Her husband, whom she met while he was an exchange student at what Updike calls the State University of New Jersey, abandoned her when Ahmad was three years old, never to be seen again; his failure to make good in America weighed heavily on his soul.

Ahmad and his mother live in New Prospect, New Jersey, a run-down postindustrial city now home mainly to blacks and immigrants. Ahmad attends the local high school, where he is of above-average scholastic ability; but, falling under the influence of Shaikh Rashid, the imam of a hole-in-the-corner mosque in New Prospect, he decides not to continue his education but to become a truck driver instead. That way he will not participate fully in the degenerate society around him. Becoming a truck driver is, for an eighteen-year-old of his intelligence and potential, like a spiritual retreat into the wilderness.

A guidance counselor at his high school, Jack Levy, a world-weary and washed-out Jew at the end of his career, tries to dissuade him from this course of action, which Levy supposes will destroy Ahmad's life chances. In the process, Levy winds up in a torrid affair with Ahmad's mother. By a coincidence of the novel's plot, the sister of Jack's wife, a woman of German Lutheran descent, is an assistant to a Donald Rumsfeld–like director of the Department of Homeland Security.

Ahmad goes to work for a cheap furniture store owned by Lebanese immigrants, whose son, called Charlie (but nonetheless a Muslim), persuades him to undertake a suicide mission to explode a bomb in the Lincoln Tunnel. Charlie is, in fact, an FBI agent who has infiltrated a band of extremists, of whom Shaikh Rashid is one; but his cover is blown and he is murdered brutally before the suicide mission can be averted. But Jack Levy, via his contact with the Department of Homeland Security, which has passed on to him information concerning the proposed bomb attack, manages to avert it by persuading Ahmad, at the last minute, to desist.

Reviewers disparaged the implausibility of the plot, whose resolution relies upon creakingly contrived coincidences, and criticized the characterization as feeble. How Ahmad became so attached to his slender Muslim heritage, for example, rather than to his much stronger Irish Catholic one—his mother being the only parent he has ever known—Updike doesn't explain at all. Perhaps he had been taunted at school for his mixed parentage and decided that he might as well die for a Muslim sheep as a Christian lamb by adopting only the Egyptian moiety of his identity; or perhaps he realized in a subliminal way that in the modern multicultural world there is more mileage in being a minority than in being a déclassé member of the mainstream. In the current climate you can't fail as a minority: you can only be failed by others.

The book's dialogue, too, is frequently stilted and unbelievable. Ahmad, for example, often sounds more like a wooden, pedantic prig than a disaffected youth emerging from a New Jersey slum, tormented by inchoate existential doubts and anxieties. For example, when Charlie tells him that his attendance at the Islamic Center had declined and that the shaikh would like to see more of him, he replies: "To chastise me, I fear. Now that I work, I neglect the Qur'an, and my Friday attendance has fallen off, though I never fail, as you have noticed, to fulfill salat, wherever I can spend five minutes in an unpolluted place." I've met a lot of eighteen-year-olds, of many different types, from the slums, but I've never heard one talk like this.

Yet for all its weaknesses, Updike's novel remains an impressive attempt to understand the worldview of a modern would-be Islamist terrorist, avoiding caricature and recognizing complexity. Without condoning terrorism and without any apologetics for those who commit it, the book invites us to see ourselves as others might see us and to look at the world through eyes other than our own. And this is surely part of the function of imaginative literature.

Updike is scarcely the first author to draw attention to the fact that terrorism is not a simple, direct response to, or result of, social injustice, poverty, or any other objectively discernible human ill.

It is not the personal that is political, but the political that is personal. People with unusually thin skins ascribe the small insults, humiliations, and setbacks consequent upon human existence to vast and malign political forces; and, projecting their own suffering onto the whole of mankind, conceive of schemes, usually involving violence, to remedy the situation that has so wounded them.

Dostoevsky knew this, but the author closest to Updike in spirit, if his great superior in felicity of execution, is Joseph Conrad, the Pole-turned-Englishman. Conrad experienced political persecution from the inside, having been exiled to Siberia during his childhood with his father by the tyrannical tsarist regime. One might have expected him therefore to have sympathized with extremists of almost any stripe, but he understood only too well that those who opposed tyranny by terrorism objected not so much to tyranny as such but to the fact that it was not they who were exercising it. Indeed, the terrorist temperament was apt to see tyranny where there was none. As Conrad puts it: "The way of even the most justifiable revolutions is prepared by personal impulses disguised into creeds."

In Conrad's *The Secret Agent*, for example, the Professor—"his title to that designation consisted in having been once assistant demonstrator in chemistry at some technical institution," who quarreled with his superiors "upon a question of unfair treatment" and who had "such an exalted conviction of his merits that it was extremely difficult for the world to treat him with justice"—is a man who has devoted himself to devising bombs and detonators. Predisposed to dissatisfaction by his small stature and unimpressive appearance, he develops "a frenzied Puritanism of ambition" that seems once again, after September 11, only too familiar to us. "The extreme, almost ascetic purity of his thought, combined with an astounding ignorance of worldly conditions, had set before him a goal of power and prestige to be attained without the medium of arts, graces, tact, wealth—by sheer weight of merit alone. . . .

"To see [his ambition] thwarted opened his eyes to the true nature of the world, whose morality was artificial, corrupt, and blasphemous. . . . By exercising his agency with ruthless defiance he procured for himself the appearances of power and personal prestige."

Updike's *Terrorist* has much in common with Conrad's *The Secret Agent*, published ninety-nine years earlier. In both books a double agent tries to get a third party to commit a bomb outrage; in both books the secret agent ends up slain. In both books the terrorists operate in a free society, unsure how far it may go in restricting freedom to protect itself from those who wish to destroy it. The terrorists in Conrad are European anarchists and socialists; in Updike they are Muslims in America: but in neither case does the righting of any "objective" injustice motivate them. They act from a mixture of personal angst and resentment, which easily attaches itself to abstract grievances about the whole of society, thus disguising the real source of their consuming but sublimated rage.

Conrad tells us that one of the sources of terrorism is laziness, or at least impatience, which is to say ambition unmatched by perseverance and tolerance of routine. Mr. Verloc, the secret agent, has a "dislike of all kinds of recognized labour," which, says Conrad, is "a temperamental defect which he shared with a large proportion of revolutionary reformers of a given social state." For—Conrad continues—"obviously one does not revolt against the advantages and opportunities of that state, but against the price which must be paid in the same coin of accepted morality, self-restraint, and toil. The majority of revolutionists are the enemies of discipline and fatigue mostly."

Ahmad's refusal to go to college might be interpreted in this light: for the path to constructive achievement is long, hard, and unsure, strewn with tedium and the chance of failure, while the life of destruction is exciting, even in its most tedious moments, because of the providential role that the destructive revolutionist has awarded himself. Once the magic wand of revolutionary destructiveness has been waved, even dull routine becomes infused with significance and excitement.

The mental laziness of Islamism, its desire that there should be to hand a ready-made solution to all the problems that mankind faces, one that is already known, and its unacknowledged fear that such a solution does not really exist, Updike captures well. When asked by his employer why he does not go for further education, Ahmad replies, "People have suggested it, sir, but I don't feel the need yet." Updike, as the omniscient narrator, adds: "More education, he feared, might weaken his faith. Doubts he held off in high school might become irresistible in college. The Straight Path was taking him in another, purer direction." The refusal of free inquiry derives from an awareness of the fragility of the basis of religious faith; and since certainty is psychologically preferable to truth, the former often being willfully mistaken for the latter, anything that threatens certainty is anathematized with fury.

Muslims are hardly the only ones, either in the past or the present, who experience difficulty in relinquishing their most cherished ideas and presuppositions. It is a normal human trait. (Darwin, in his *Autobiography*, tells us that when he came across a fact that threw some doubt upon the theory he was developing, he wrote it down, for otherwise he was sure to forget it.) But when a system of ideas and set beliefs claims eternal validity and infallibility, when people adopt that system as their primary source of identity, and when into the bargain those people find themselves in a position of long-standing and seemingly irreversible technical and economic inferiority and dependence vis-à-vis people with very different ideas and beliefs, resentment is certain to result. Not wishing to relinquish their cherished ideology—their only possible source of collective pride and accomplishment—they seek to explain the technical and economic superiority of others by different kinds of denigratory mental maneuvers. They may claim, for example, that the West has achieved its preeminence by illicit use of force and pillage, by exploiting and appropriating the oil of the Muslim lands, say.

The justice of a criticism does not depend upon the motive that lies behind it, of course. But the claim about the exploitation of oil is not merely self-serving; it is patently absurd. If anything, the direction of the exploitation has been precisely the opposite, for merely by virtue of their fortunate geographical location, and with scarcely any effort on their part, the people of the Arabian peninsula and elsewhere have enjoyed a high standard of living thanks entirely to the ingenuity of those whom they accuse of exploitation and without whom the oil resource would not be an economic resource at all.

But this fact does not mean that all Muslim criticism of the West is entirely wrong or beside the point. Updike begins his novel with a description of the world as Ahmad sees it, and a most uncomplimentary vision it is. What he sees is a world of brutal ugliness, vulgarity, egotism, and lack of restraint. He sees a civilization that is charmless and lacking in refinement and substance, even if the people living in it seem to be enjoying themselves at least some of the time. Their sorrows, however, are the consequence of their enjoyments, and outweigh them; their horizons are severely limited to the eternal present moment.

"All day long [at Central High School] girls sway and sneer," exposing their "bare bellies, adorned with navel studs and low-down purple tattoos," while "boys strut and saunter along and look dead-eyed, indicating with their killer gestures and careless scornful laughs that this world is all there is." An atmosphere of indulgence pervades the school. "The halls of the high school smell of perfume and bodily exhalations, of chewing gum and impure cafeteria food, and of cloth—cotton and wool and the synthetic materials of running shoes warmed by young flesh. Between classes there is a thunder of movement; the noise is stretched thin over a violence beneath, barely restrained."

Out in the run-down city, "former display windows [are] covered by plywood crawling with spray-painted graffiti." What do these graffiti mean? "To Ahmad's eyes, the bulbous letters of the graffiti, their boasts of gang affiliation, assert an importance to which their perpetrators have pathetically little other claim. Sinking into a morass of Godlessness, lost young men proclaim, by means of property defacement, an identity." The teachers at the school, weak or unbelieving Christians and Jews, preach restraint to the children without really believing in anything much themselves, and without practicing such restraint in their private lives. Tylenol Jones, a young black who takes an instant and violent dislike to Ahmad (in a society, or aggregation, of individualists and egotists, people dislike those who are very different from themselves), perfectly symbolizes the generalized egotism of society: he received his name merely because his mother happened to see a television advertisement for the product and liked the sound. Whimsical rejection of convention could scarcely go further; and such a rejection reduces freedom to nothing more than the practical expression of the first thing that comes into one's head, even if it is at the expense of another human being. As such, freedom seems to Ahmad to be not a blessing but a curse.

Reviewers have mocked and even reviled Updike for his unappetizing description, through the eyes of Ahmad, of the popular culture of underclass America, and for pointing to revulsion against it as a motive for a suicide bombing. Even if one allows that Updike's description is accurate (as I think any tolerably objective observer must), it is in fact so partial a characterization of the country in its entirety as to be utterly tendentious. It is to mistake the part for the whole, and it risks suggesting that Islamist bombers might have a point after all. Besides, there are far worse things in the world than the smell of chewing gum and bad cafeteria food, and far worse acts committed than the adornment of walls and other surfaces with ugly, hermetic, and no doubt idiotic signs. To complain seriously of what amounts to bad taste and make it a motive for mass murder, when the crimes of Hitler, Stalin, Mao, and Pol Pot are still within living memory, is—well, in bad taste.

But it seems to me that Updike rather than his critics is right—or rather, accurate. He is not trying to justify Ahmad but to explain him. How could Ahmad have developed a more rounded view of the social environment into which he was born, or have achieved some kind of mature historical perspective on it, without the aid and guidance of people who knew better, whose mental world was not circumscribed by New Prospect, New Jersey? His mother is unable or disinclined to provide him with any guidance. To understand the distinction between criticism of the way people choose to use their freedom and criticism of freedom itself requires some historical and philosophical sophistication, which it is the duty of schools to inculcate. By inference, Central High School has failed to do this where Ahmad is concerned, leaving his clever but uncritical mind a fallow field in which Shaikh Rashid can plant his ill-germinating seeds.

The crude nostrums of Islamism rush in where the Enlightenment fears to tread.

I have talked to a lot of young Muslim critics of Western society, living in the West, and few of them were aware of the philosophical basis of Western achievement, which they believed to be merely materialist and founded on crude plunder, never having heard any other viewpoint.

Updike also has an understanding of the role of sexuality in the formation of the Islamist terrorist mind-set. On the very first page Ahmad demonstrates that he is a sexual being who is struggling to control his desires, because he realizes that when unbridled or uncontrolled, sexuality is dehumanizing. The description of the navel studs and purple tattoos lying low on the abdomen ends with his question: "What else is there to see?" Clearly he can imagine it and be attracted by it.

Later in the novel, a black girl called Joryleen, whom he knew at school, has since become a prostitute with Tylenol Jones as her pimp, and she seduces Ahmad to the point where she masturbates him to orgasm. He is not so very different, and has never been so very different, at least in his basic desires, from the mass of his fellow slum dwellers, whom he has hitherto despised and excoriated. He is attracted by what is repellent to him; his rejection of the society that produces such powerful attractants is what psychiatrists used to call, in the days when Freud was still a respectable figure, reaction formation. In resisting the hypersexuality of his environment, he is trapped into falsely denying his sexuality altogether.

All in all, then, Updike has produced a more convincing and subtle and, in my view, accurate portrait of a young Islamist terrorist than he has generally received credit for—even for all his book's literary faults. He rightly sees Islamism in the West as culturally hybrid rather than as a pure product of Islam: a reaction, albeit one consonant with certain Islamic traditions, to a very severe and, indeed, overwhelming cultural challenge from without rather than as something arising purely or spontaneously from within Islam itself. He understands the deeply human but also deeply destructive desire for a simple solution to all existential and practical problems at once. He is sufficiently imaginative to understand that our imperfect societies have more than enough within them to appall sensitive outsiders and marginals (as surely all conservatives should appreciate). He also realizes that violent repulsion can be the consequence of illicit attraction. And all this without for a moment suggesting that Islamic terrorism is other than a terrible scourge.

This is quite an achievement, even if his book will not outlive the Islamist threat, as Conrad's book has outlived the anarchist one.

2006

Suicide Bombers

◆ ALL TERRORISTS, presumably, know the dangers that they run, accepting them as an occupational hazard; given Man's psychological makeup—or at least the psychological makeup of certain young men—these dangers may act as an attraction, not a deterrent. But only a few terrorists use their own deaths as an integral means of terrorizing others. They seem to be a breed apart, with whom the rest of humanity can have little or nothing in common.

Certainly they sow panic more effectively than other terrorists. Those who leave bombs in public places and then depart, despicable as they are, presumably still have attachments to their own lives and therefore may be open to dissuasion or negotiation. By contrast, no threat (at first sight) might deter someone who is prepared to extinguish himself to advance his cause, and who considers such self-annihilation while killing as many strangers as possible a duty, an honor, and a merit that will win ample rewards in the hereafter. And Britain has suddenly been forced to acknowledge that it has an unknown number of such people in its midst, some of them homegrown.

The mere contemplation of a suicide bomber's state of mind is deeply unsettling, even without considering its practical consequences. I have met a would-be suicide bomber who had not yet had the chance to put his thanatological daydream into practice. What could possibly have produced as embittered a mentality as his—what experience of life, what thoughts, what doctrines? What fathomless depths of self-pity led him to the conclusion that only by killing himself and others could he give a noble and transcendent meaning to his existence?

As is by now well known (for the last few years have made us more attentive to Islamic concepts and ways of thinking, irrespective of their intrinsic worth), the term "jihad" has two meanings: inner struggle and holy war. While the political meaning connotes violence, though with such supposed justifications as the defense of Islam and the spread of the faith among the heathen, the personal meaning generally suggests something peaceful and inward-looking. The struggle this kind of jihad entails is spiritual; it is the effort to overcome the internal obstacles—above all, forbidden desires—that prevents the good Muslim from achieving complete submission to God's will. Commentators have tended to see this type of jihad as harmless or even as beneficial—a kind of self-improvement that leads to decency, respectability, good behavior, and material success.

In Britain, however, these two forms of jihad have coalesced in a most murderous fashion. Those who died in the 2005 London bombings were sacrificial victims to the need of four young men to resolve a conflict deep within themselves (and within many young Muslims), and they imagined they could do so only by the most extreme possible interpretation of their ancestral religion.

Young Muslim men in Britain—as in France and elsewhere in the West—have a problem of personal, cultural, and national identity. They are deeply secularized, with little religious faith, even if most will admit to a belief in God. Their interest in Islam is slight. They do not pray or keep Ramadan (except if it brings them some practical advantage, such as the postponement of a court appearance). Their tastes are for the most part those of non-Muslim lower-class young men. They dress indistinguishably from their white and black contemporaries, and affect the same hairstyles and mannerisms, including the vulpine lope of the slums. Gold chains, the heavier the better, and gold front teeth, without dental justification, are symbols of their success in the streets, which is to say of illicit enrichment.

Many young Muslims, unlike the sons of Hindus and Sikhs who immigrated into Britain at the same time as their parents, take drugs, including heroin. They drink, indulge in casual sex, and make nightclubs the focus of their lives. Work and careers are at best a painful necessity, a slow and inferior means of obtaining the money for their distractions.

But if in many respects their tastes and behavior are indistinguishable from those of underclass white males, there are nevertheless clear and important differences. Most obviously, whatever the similarity between them and their white counterparts in their taste for sex, drugs, and rock and roll, they nevertheless do not mix with young white men, even in the neighborhoods devoted to the satisfaction of their tastes. They are in parallel with the whites rather than intersecting with them.

Another obvious difference is the absence of young Muslim women from the resorts of mass distraction. However similar young Muslim men might be in their tastes to young white men, they would be horrified, and indeed turn extremely violent, if their sisters comported themselves as young white women do. They satisfy their sexual needs with prostitutes and those whom they quite openly call "white sluts." (Many a young white female patient of mine has described being taunted in this fashion as she walked through a street inhabited by Muslims.) And, of course, they do not have to suffer much sexual frustration in an environment where people decide on sexual liaisons within seconds of acquaintance.

However secular the tastes of the young Muslim men, they strongly wish to maintain the male dominance they have inherited from their parents. A sister who has the temerity to choose a boyfriend for herself, or who even expresses a desire for an independent social life, is likely to suffer a beating, followed by surveillance of Stasi-like thoroughness. The young men instinctively understand that their inherited system of male domination—which provides them, by means of forced marriage, with sexual gratification at home while simultaneously freeing them from domestic chores and allowing them to live completely Westernized lives outside the home, including further sexual adventures into which their wives cannot inquire—is strong but brittle, rather as communism was: it is an all-or-nothing phenomenon, and every breach must meet swift punishment.

Even if for no other reason, then (and there are in fact other reasons), young Muslim males have a strong motive for maintaining an identity apart. And since people rarely like to admit low motives for their behavior, such as the wish to maintain a self-gratifying dominance, these young Muslims need a more elevated justification for their conduct toward women. They find it, of course, in a residual Islam: not the Islam of onerous duties, rituals, and prohibitions, which interferes so insistently in day-to-day life, but in an Islam of residual feeling, which allows them a sense of moral superiority to everything around them, including women, without in any way cramping their style.

This Islam contains little that is theological, spiritual, or even religious, but it nevertheless exists in the mental economy as what anatomists call a "potential space." A potential space occurs where two tissues or organs are separated by smooth membranes that are normally close together but that can be separated by an accumulation of fluid such as pus if infection or inflammation occurs. And, of course, such inflammation readily occurs in the minds of young men who easily believe themselves to be ill-used, and who have been raised on the thin gruel of popular Western culture without an awareness that any other kind of Western culture exists.

The dissatisfactions of young Muslim men in Britain are manifold. Most will experience at some time slighting or downright insulting remarks about them or their group—the word "Paki" is a term of disdainful abuse—and these experiences tend to grow in severity and significance with constant rehearsal in the mind as it seeks an external explanation for its woes. Minor tribulations thus swell into major injustices, which in turn explain the evident failure of Muslims to rise in their adopted land. The French-Iranian researcher Farhad Khosrokhavar, who interviewed fifteen French Muslim prisoners convicted of planning terrorist acts, relates in his book *Suicide Bombers: Allah's New Martyrs* how some of his interviewees had been converted to the terrorist outlook by a single insulting remark—for example, when one of their sisters was called a "dirty Arab" when she explained how she couldn't leave home on her own as other girls could. Such is the fragility of the modern ego—not of Muslims alone but of countless people brought up in our modern culture of ineffable self-importance, in which an insult is understood not as an inevitable human annoyance but as a wound that outweighs all the rest of one's experience.

The evidence of Muslims' own eyes and of their own lives, as well as that of statistics, is quite clear: Muslim immigrants and their descendants are more likely to be poor, to live in overcrowded conditions, to be unemployed, to have low levels of educational achievement, and above all to be imprisoned than other South Asian immigrants and their descendants. The refusal to educate females to their full capacity is a terrible handicap in a society in which, perhaps regrettably, prosperity requires two household incomes. The idea that one is already in possession of the final revealed truth, leading to an inherently superior way of life, inhibits adaptation to a technically more advanced society. Even so, some British Muslims do succeed (the father of one of the London bombers owned two shops, two houses, and drove a new Mercedes)—a fact that their compatriots interpret exactly backward: not that Muslims can succeed, but that generally they can't, because British society is inimical to Muslims.

In coming to this conclusion, young Muslims would only be adopting the logic that has driven Western social policy for so long: that any difference in economic and social outcome between groups is the result of social injustice and adverse discrimination. The premises of multiculturalism don't even permit asking whether reasons internal to the groups themselves might account for differences in outcomes.

The BBC peddles this sociological view consistently. In 1997, for example, it stated that Muslims "continue to face discrimination," as witness the fact that they were three times as likely to be unemployed long-term as West Indians; and this has been its line ever since. If more Muslims than any other group possess no educational qualifications whatsoever, even though the hurdles for winning such qualifications have constantly fallen, it can only be because of discrimination—though a quarter of all medical students in Britain are now of Indian subcontinental descent. It can have nothing whatever to do with the widespread—and illegal—practice of refusing to allow girls to continue at school, which the press scarcely ever mentions, and which the educational authorities rarely if ever investigate. If youth unemployment among Muslims is two and a half times the rate among whites, it can be only because of discrimination—though youth unemployment among Hindus is actually lower than among whites (and this even though many young Hindus complain of being mistaken for Muslims). And so on and so on.

A constant and almost unchallenged emphasis on "social justice," the negation of which is, of course, "discrimination," can breed only festering embitterment. Where the definition of justice is entitlement by virtue of group existence rather than reward for individual effort, a radical overhaul of society will appear necessary to achieve such justice. Islamism in Britain is thus not the product of Islam alone: it is the product of the meeting of Islam with a now deeply entrenched native mode of thinking about social problems.

And it is here that the "potential space" of Islamism, with its ready-made diagnosis and prescriptions, opens up and fills with the pus of implacable hatred for many in search of a reason for and a solution to their discontents. According to Islamism, the West can never meet the demands of justice because it is decadent, materialistic, individualistic, heathen, and democratic rather than theocratic. Only a return to the principles and practices of seventh-century Arabia will resolve all personal and political problems at the same time. This notion is fundamentally no more (and no less) bizarre or stupid than the Marxist notion that captivated so many Western intellectuals throughout the twentieth century: that the abolition of private property would lead to final and lasting harmony among men. Both conceptions offer a formula that, rigidly followed, would resolve all human problems.

Of course the Islamic formula holds no attraction for young women in the West. A recent survey for the French interior ministry found that 83 percent of Muslim converts and reconverts (that is, secularized Muslims who adopted Salafism) in France were men; and from my clinical experience I would bet that the 17 percent of converts who were women converted in the course of a love affair rather than on account of what Edward Gibbon, in another context, called "the evident truth of the doctrine itself."

The West is a formidable enemy, however, difficult to defeat, for it exists not only in the cities, the infrastructure, and the institutions of Europe and America but in the hearts and minds even of those who oppose it and wish to destroy it. The London bombers were as much products of the West as of Islam; their tastes and their desires were largely Westernized. The bombers dressed no differently from other young men from the slums; and in every culture, appearance is part, at least, of identity. In British inner cities in particular, what you wear is nine-tenths of what you are.

But the Western identity goes far deeper. One of the bombers was a young man of West Indian descent whose half-sister (in his milieu, full siblings are almost unknown) reports that he was a "normal" boy, impassioned by rap music until the age of fifteen, when he converted to Islam. It need hardly be pointed out that rap music—full of inchoate rage, hatred, and intemperance—does not instill a balanced or subtle understanding of the world in its listeners. It fills and empties the mind at the same time: fills it with debased notions and empties it of critical faculties. The qualities of mind and character that are attracted to it, and that consider it an art form worthy of time and attention, are not so easily overcome or replaced. Jermaine Lindsay was only nineteen, four years into his conversion from rap to Islam, when he died—an age at which impulsivity is generally at its greatest, requiring the kind of struggle for self-mastery that rap music is dedicated to undermining. Islam would have taught him to hate and despise what he had been, but he must have been aware that he still was what he had been. To a hatred of the world, his conversion added a self-hatred.

The other bombers had passions for soccer, cricket, and pop music. They gave no indication of religious fanaticism before their dreadful deeds, and their journeys to Pakistan—in retrospect, indications of a growing indoctrination by fundamentalism—could have seemed at the time merely family visits. In the meantime they led highly Westernized lives, availing themselves of all the products of Western ingenuity to which Muslims have contributed nothing for centuries. It is, in fact, literally impossible for modern Muslims to expunge the West from their lives: it enters the fabric of their existence at every turn. Osama bin Laden himself is utterly dependent upon the West for his weaponry, his communications, his travel, and his funds. He speaks of the West's having stolen Arabian oil, but of what use would oil have been to the Arabs if it had remained under their sands, as it would have done without the intervention of the

West? Without the West, what fortune would bin Laden's family have made from what construction in Saudi Arabia?

Muslims who reject the West are therefore engaged in a losing and impossible inner jihad, or struggle, to expunge everything that is not Muslim from their breasts. It can't be done, for their technological and scientific dependence is necessarily also a cultural one. You can't believe in a return to seventh-century Arabia as being all-sufficient for human requirements and at the same time drive around in a brand-new red Mercedes, as one of the London bombers did shortly before his murderous suicide. An awareness of the contradiction must gnaw in even the dullest fundamentalist brain.

Furthermore fundamentalists must be sufficiently self-aware to know that they will never be willing to forgo the appurtenances of Western life: the taste for them is too deeply implanted in their souls, too deeply a part of what they are as human beings, ever to be eradicated. It is possible to reject isolated aspects of modernity but not modernity itself. Whether they like it or not, Muslim fundamentalists are modern men—modern men trying, impossibly, to be something else.

They therefore have at least a nagging intimation that their chosen utopia is not really a utopia at all: that deep within themselves there exists something that makes it unachievable and even undesirable. How to persuade themselves and others that their lack of faith, their vacillation, is really the strongest possible faith? What more convincing evidence of faith could there be than to die for its sake? How can a person be really attached or attracted to rap music and cricket and Mercedes cars if he is prepared to blow himself up as a means of destroying the society that produces them? Death will be the end of the illicit attachment that he cannot entirely eliminate from his heart.

The two forms of jihad, the inner and the outer, the greater and the lesser, thus coalesce in one apocalyptic action. By means of suicide bombing, the bombers overcome moral impurities and religious doubts within themselves and, supposedly, strike an external blow for the propagation of the faith.

Of course, hatred is the underlying emotion. A man in prison who told me that he wanted to be a suicide bomber was more hate-filled than any man I have ever met. The offspring of a broken marriage between a Muslim man and a female convert, he had followed the trajectory of many young men in his area: sex and drugs and rock and roll, untainted by anything resembling higher culture. Violent and aggressive by nature, intolerant of the slightest frustration to his will and frequently suicidal, he had experienced taunting during his childhood because of his mixed parentage. After a vicious rape for which he went to prison, he converted to a Salafist form of Islam and became convinced that any system of justice that could take the word of a mere woman over his own was irredeemably corrupt.

I noticed one day that his mood had greatly improved; he was communicative and almost jovial, which he had never been before. I asked him what had changed in his life for the better. He had made his decision, he said. Everything was resolved. He was not going to kill himself in an isolated way, as he had previously intended. Suicide was a mortal sin, according to the tenets of the Islamic faith. No, when he got out of prison he would not kill himself; he would make himself a martyr, and be rewarded eternally, by making himself into a bomb and taking as many enemies with him as he could.

Enemies? I asked; what enemies? How could he know that the people he killed at random would be enemies? They were enemies, he said, because they lived happily in our rotten and unjust society. Therefore, by definition, they were enemies— enemies in the objective sense, as Stalin might have put it—and hence were legitimate targets.

I asked him whether he thought that, in order to deter him from his course of action, it would be right for the state to threaten to kill his mother and his brothers and sisters—and to carry out this threat if he carried out his, in order to deter others like him.

The idea appalled him, not because it was yet another example of the wickedness of a Western democratic state but because he could not conceive of such a state acting in this unprincipled way. In other words, he assumed a high degree of moral restraint on the part of the very organism that he wanted to attack and destroy.

Of course, one of the objects of the bombers, instinctive rather than articulated, might be to undermine this very restraint, both of the state and of the population itself, in order to reveal to the majority of Muslims the true evil nature of the society in which they live, and force them into the camp of the extremists. If so, there is some hope of success: physical attacks on Muslims (or on Hindus and Sikhs ignorantly taken to be Muslims) increased in Britain by six times in the immediate aftermath of the bombings, according to the police. It wouldn't take many more such bombings, perhaps, to provoke real and serious intercommunal violence on the Indian subcontinental model. Britain teems with aggressive, violent subgroups who would be only too delighted to make pogroms a reality.

Even if there is no such dire an eventuality, the outlook is sufficiently grim and without obvious solution. A highly secularized Muslim population whose men nevertheless wish to maintain their dominance over women and need a justification for doing so; the hurtful experience of disdain or rejection from the surrounding society; the bitter disappointment of a frustrated materialism and a seemingly perpetual inferior status in the economic hierarchy; the extreme insufficiency and unattractiveness of modern popular culture that is without value; the readiness to hand of an ideological and religious solution that is flattering to self-esteem and allegedly all-sufficient, and yet in unavoidable conflict with a large element of each individual's identity; an oscillation between feelings of inferiority and superiority, between humiliation about that which is Western and that which is non-Western in the self; and the grotesque inflation of the importance of personal existential problems that is typical of modern individualism—all ensure fertile ground for the recruitment of further "martyrs" for years to come.

Surveys suggest that between 6 and 13 percent of British Muslims—that is, between 98,000 and 208,000 people—are sympathetic toward Islamic terrorists and their efforts. Theoretical sympathy expressed in a survey is not the same thing as active support or a wish to emulate the "martyrs" in person, of course. But it is nevertheless a sufficient proportion and absolute number of sympathizers to make suspicion and hostility toward Muslims by the rest of society not entirely irrational, though such suspicion and hostility could easily increase support for extremism. This is the tightrope that the British state and population will now have to walk for the foreseeable future; and the sweet dream of universal cultural compatibility has been replaced, in a single day, by the nightmare of permanent conflict.

2005

Multiculturalism Starts Losing Its Luster

◈ MULTICULTURALISM rests on the supposition—or better, the dishonest pretense—that all cultures are equal and that no fundamental conflict can arise between the customs, mores, and philosophical outlooks of two different cultures. The multiculturalist preaches that, in an age of mass migration, society can (and should) be a kind of salad bowl, a receptacle for wonderful exotic ingredients from around the world, the more the better, each bringing its special flavor to the cultural mix. For the salad to be delicious, no ingredient should predominate and impose its flavor on the others.

Even as a culinary metaphor, this view is wrong: every cook knows that not every ingredient blends with every other. But the spread and influence of an idea is by no means necessarily proportional to its intrinsic worth, including (perhaps especially) among those who gain their living by playing with ideas, the intelligentsia.

Reality, though, has a way of revenging itself upon the frivolous, and September 11 has seemingly concentrated minds a little. Some signs indicate that in Britain the pieties of multiculturalism, for years an official orthodoxy, are beginning to face a challenge.

The Home Secretary, David Blunkett, for example, recently declaimed that immigrants to Britain should learn English. Blunkett made this heterodox suggestion in response to riotous clashes in northern England between white youths and Muslim youths of Pakistani descent. Liberals predictably decried his comments as tactless at best and protofascist at worst. Didn't they give succor to the vicious xenophobic elements in British society, perhaps even portending a new dark age of intolerance?

In fact Blunkett's remarks were both on and off the mark. Doubtless all of the rioting Muslim youths spoke English. Hardly any British-born young men and women of South Asian descent do not speak it—though some, given the undemanding British school system, speak it poorly. So it is not true, as Blunkett implied, that a failure to learn English was to blame for the rioters' aggrieved sense of being unequal citizens in British society.

Yet Blunkett was right in other respects. Though the rioting youths could speak English, the brides they would bring back from Pakistan would not—and, furthermore, never would. Many women I have encountered as patients who came to Britain from Pakistan thirty years ago, at age sixteen or eighteen, still know little English—but not from any unwillingness to learn. Their husbands actively prevented them from learning the language, to make sure that they would stay enclosed in a ghetto and not get any ideas above their station. The same rioting youths who protested British society's failure to accept them as equal citizens have themselves sought to reproduce the unequal social patterns of rural Pakistan, half a world away, because it suited them to do so.

Multiculturalism encourages this stance. If all cultures are equal, and none has the right to impose its standards on any other, what is wrong with the immigrant ghettos that have emerged, where the population (that is to say, the male population) enjoys, de facto, extraterritorial rights? If it is the custom of their ancestral culture to keep girls out of school and force them into marriages that they do not want and to confiscate the passports that the British government issues them for their personal use, what can a multiculturalist object to without asserting the superiority of his own values?

Giving further weight to Blunkett's remarks is the silliness of the government language practices that multiculturalism has spawned. For example, one can take the driver's license test in Britain in a startling variety of languages. Spoken instructions come even in the various dialects of Albanian, Kurdish, and Lingala. For the written part, test takers need not know how to read the Latin alphabet (that would be discriminatory): officials provide the questions in the script of your choice. Never mind that traffic signs are still in English.

Nor is the driver's test anomalous. Government pamphlets, including those concerning health and social security benefits, now routinely appear in myriad languages—at public expense. When I went to vote in the local elections not long ago, I saw notices in various Indian languages and in Vietnamese explaining how to cast a vote. And at my local airport, the sign directing travelers to the line for returning British passport holders is written not only in English, but in Bengali, Hindi, Punjabi, and Urdu (each with its own script): proof that the granting of citizenship requires no proficiency in the national language.

These practices send the message that newcomers to Britain have no obligation to learn English—indeed, that the obligation is the other way around: that the British state must make itself clear in Arabic, Farsi, Russian, Somali, Swahili, and many other languages. British officialdom doubtless does not know that the confusion of languages after the Tower of Babel fell was meant as a punishment.

In today's multicultural climate the general population, it seems, has the duty to be familiar with the immigrant tongues too. My local public schools now teach Bengali and Urdu, so that the "local" (i.e., white) population may learn to mix better with the immigrant population. While I have no objection to the children of immigrants speaking their parents' native tongue at home, or to the private decision of anyone to master any language he chooses, a private choice is very different from the government's ideological decision to offer such languages (of minor global importance) in the state schools. How not to see such a decision as deliberately subversive of belief in the primacy of European culture—with which, after all, the immigrants have chosen to throw in their lot?

Clumsy as Blunkett may have been, then, he has drawn attention to an important issue—one that makes clear what an absurd and at heart insincere doctrine multiculturalism is. Yet it is also a dangerous doctrine, inspiring policies certain to maintain minorities in their impoverishment, stoke their resentment, and exacerbate racial tensions—while providing employment for a growing number of bureaucrats.

Another Blairite who once uncritically espoused multicultural pieties has recently undergone a conversion: Commission for Racial Equality chairman Trevor Phillips. In an interview with the London *Times*, Phillips, a black born in Guyana, argued that England should abandon the whole concept of multiculturalism since it was doing more harm than good. Officials should even stop using the word itself, he added.

Phillips noted that Britain has a long and mostly distinguished history of accepting people to its shores and integrating them into its national life, while at the same time deriving benefits from whatever skills they may have brought with them. Britishness has been a cultural, not a racial or biological, concept with a tradition of tolerance, compromise, civility, gentlemanly reserve, respect for privacy, individuality (evident as far back as Chaucer's time), a ready acceptance of and even affection for eccentricity, a belief in the rule of law, a profound sense of irony, and a desire for fair play: in short, the common decency that Orwell wrote of so eloquently.

Utopian intellectuals, including the theorists of multiculturalism, deride many of these now-weakened British characteristics, on the grounds that they were never universal among the population (but what characteristics are?) and had more drawbacks than advantages. But Britain's common decency proved self-evident to generations of immigrants and refugees, among them my mother, who, arriving in Britain from Germany in 1938, noticed them instantly, to her relief and great admiration.

My family history attests further to British society's generous capacity to absorb. My father, whose immigrant parents never learned to speak English well, attended a slum school during and just after World War I, with classmates so poor that they went hungry and barefoot. Despite his background, my father found himself inducted into British culture by teachers who did not believe that the ability to understand and appreciate Milton or Shakespeare, or to make a contribution to national life, depended on social class or required roots in the soil going back before the Norman conquest. His teachers had the same faith in the liberating power of high culture, in its universal value and appeal, that many British workers then shared. As the historian Jonathan Rose has beautifully demonstrated in *The Intellectual Life of the British Working Classes*, many ordinary English workingmen, who led lives of sometimes numbing toil and financial hardship, nevertheless devoted much of their little spare time and tiny wages to improving their lives by strenuous reading of good literature, of whose transcendent value they had no doubt—a faith borne out by the success many of them attained in later years.

My father's teachers were the only people I ever heard him mention with unqualified admiration and gratitude. And he was right to do so: their philosophy was infinitely more generous than that of the multiculturalists who succeeded them. They had no desire to enclose my father in the world that his parents had fled. And they understood that for society to avoid bitter internal conflicts, everyone had to share important elements of culture and historical knowledge that would result in a shared identity. Not by chance did Trevor Phillips regret eighty years later that teachers were instructing children less and less in the great works of English literature, especially Shakespeare—a deprivation wrought not because teachers were complying with any spontaneous demand from below but because they were implementing the theories of elite educationists, especially the multiculturalists.

Phillips rightly pointed out that English literature is the perfect vehicle for promoting a shared identity. Not to teach Shakespeare or other giants of British culture is to provide no worthwhile tradition with which the increasingly diverse population can identify. Without such a tradition, nothing deeper than the ephemeral products of popular culture will be on hand to unite that population, even as profound cultural differences divide it. A shared culture consisting of nothing but pop ephemera will likely arouse the justified contempt of immigrants and their children, driving them into ethnic, cultural, or ideological enclaves in search of something more mentally and spiritually nourishing— thereby increasing social tensions, sometimes disastrously.

The shared identity that my father's teachers believed in was not an imposed uniformity, as present-day critics allege; they did not seek to turn out mental clones. Far from it. Part of that shared identity—a source of pride—was inventiveness and freedom of thought, the permission for the mind to voyage forever on strange seas of thought alone (as Wordsworth described Newton). And this shared identity relieved those who participated in it of the need to cling too strongly to other, potentially conflicting, identities. The national identity was strong but loose, permitting a great deal of personal freedom and give-and-take—much more so, usually, than the ethnic identities that immigrants bring with them. Freedom of religious belief was complete, as was practice, provided that it complied with the law and claimed no special privileges for itself. Induction into British culture did not fetter or circumscribe the immigrant, therefore, any more than speaking English determines what anyone has to say.

Britain's openness is precisely what made it so attractive to immigrants. While by no means without blemish, Britain's history of openness (compared with most societies) goes back a long way, and it has allowed many groups of newcomers to become national assets. The Huguenots, for example, immensely enriched British cultural and economic life. Before their arrival, all silk in Britain came from France; after their arrival, most French silk came from Britain. In time the Huguenots became intensely British—is any writer more British than De Quincey?—but for many years they had their own churches, and some spoke French at home until well into the nineteenth century.

It was this tradition of integration that Phillips eloquently invoked in his interview. Since the chairmen of quasi-governmental bodies such as his are not known for speaking courageously out of turn, his words most likely reflected the thinking of the government, alarmed at the extent of sympathy in the Muslim population for the September 11 terrorists.

Phillips failed to mention one vital difference between previous and contemporary influxes into Britain, however. The relative tolerance and flexibility that he praises were spontaneous, informal, and undirected, without official interference. It simply never occurred to anyone in my father's day that the children of immigrants should or would have a fundamentally different culture from that of the larger population, or that they would have any cultural peculiarities or sensibilities that needed catering to. They would be British without qualification. These immigrants, of course, arrived during a prolonged era of national self-confidence, when Britain was either a rising or a risen power. The generosity of my father's teachers grew out of pride in their culture and country.

Since then, much has changed. We live in a time of deep mistrust of spontaneous, undirected social processes—a mistrust of which Phillips's organization is one symptom. The Commission for Racial Equality that he chairs believes that racial prejudice and unfairness can only be eradicated if the government ceaselessly monitors racial statistics for inequalities (several organizations that I belong to repeatedly try to extract from me my "ethnic" group, though I refuse to answer). Paradoxically, the commission simultaneously denies, at least in theory, any underlying reality to the racial and ethnic categories into which it divides people for monitoring purposes, since it takes for granted that any low levels in achievement among the monitored racial groups must result from prejudice alone, not from any differences in the attitude or behavior of those groups. Without official bureaucratic interference, in this view, society will remain mired in racial prejudice. Minorities will stagnate or even retrogress.

In addition, confidence in Britain's historical and cultural record, as embodying anything worthwhile, let alone uniquely valuable, has all but vanished. Those things that the nation once glorified, it now derides and satirizes. Not so long ago the prime minister attacked the very notion that the British past held anything worth preserving, the "forces of conservatism" being for him a synonym for evil. Reality has, belatedly, taught him otherwise.

No doubt the shift in attitude partly results from the collapse of British power and the nation's long retreat from world importance. But it also results from the growth of the intellectual class, whose livelihood depends on ceaseless carping. Thanks to the intellectuals, for instance, the teaching of history has become an ideological minefield, with grievance groups demanding that their ancestors' suffering enjoy special status in the narrative. And if British history and culture are nothing but the story of internal and external oppression, of injustice and exploitation, why should those who come to these shores learn our national traditions and culture? Much better for them just to keep their own. One professor of race relations, Bikhu Parekh, has even suggested that Britain should change its name, which has so many negative historical connotations for millions around the world. Now that Britain has become so ineradicably multicultural, he says, there is no justification for it to be "British" any more.

Such fatuities are likely, and perhaps are intended, to produce an extreme reaction from the native-born population, demonstrating that the original contention was correct: that the British tradition is simply one of violent intolerance and oppression—from which we need such luminaries as the professor, wielding coercive administrative powers, to deliver us.

A new mass immigration to Britain from every region of the globe, in which the differences between the immigrants and the host population are profound, has occurred precisely at the moment when the multiculturalists have helped undermine the capacity of British culture to absorb them, in the hope that "a community of communities" (to use Parekh's phrase) would emerge: in short, that the lion of the Somali tribal ethic would somehow lie down with the lamb of the British law.

To be sure, many people flee their homelands to live under our rule of law. Among my patients are some refugees, most of them people of intelligence, drive, and clear-sightedness. They have no doubts about the benefits of the rule of law, having experienced the opposite in their own flesh and blood. They know what a relief it is not to fear the nocturnal knock at the door and to pass a man in uniform without trembling with anxiety.

They know also that the rule of law is an historical achievement, not the natural state of man. It is a pleasure to hear my refugee patients descant on that great historical achievement.

Because of their own experience, they do not take it for granted. They know that it arose from a long philosophical and political development, one unique in world history. They know that it is a fragile achievement and easily destroyed.

Recently a highly intelligent Iranian refugee consulted me. The medical part of the consultation over, we began to chat about Iranian affairs. He was a political philosopher not by training or inclination but by experience and necessity. He felt that, in the end, the clerical regime had done an immense service to the cause of political secularism in Iran, because even previously religious people now deeply opposed clerical rule. The clerics had done more damage to the cause of Islam among the Iranian population by their brutality and corruption than the infidels could ever inflict. His problem, of course, was that he lived in the personal short term, not the historical long run.

He appreciated deeply the British institutions that now protected him. He had experienced occasional hostility from individual Britons, but he realized that it was the product of ineradicable human nature, not of official malice. Above all, he said, Britain had a different history from Iran's—of struggle no doubt, but also of compromise—which allowed us to take our liberty for granted (a dangerous thing to do). It was, he said, a very valuable and inspiring history. What impressed him first when he arrived was how everyone just assumed that he could say what he liked, without fear of retribution—a freedom above price. But he recognized that he could only be part of that worthy society if he chose to fit in, abandoning any aspects of his Iranian culture incompatible with it, which he was only too happy to do. The fundamental demands and responsibilities, he felt, were upon the immigrant, not upon the host country.

It would be vain to suggest that all immigrants are as conscious of these demands and responsibilities as he. And if we are to avoid violently disaffected and resentful ethnic enclaves in our midst, we need to teach immigrants that the freedom, prosperity, and tolerance they enjoy result from a long spiritual and cultural development, not to be taken for granted, and that they have a magnificence and grandeur.

In the modern multicultural climate, though, there is no quick way of doing this. Because of the ideological cacophony that drowns out this cardinal, though obvious, message, it is impossible to relay it unself-consciously, as my father's teachers had done. Nor would one wish the message to harden into an official dogma: the answer to a false orthodoxy is not another orthodoxy that denies contrary evidence. We must persuade, not coerce or indoctrinate, and to do so we must first disabuse our intellectuals of the notion—frivolous but damaging—that society should be a cultural salad.

2004

In the Asylum

◆ THE VICTORIAN lunatic asylums of my city were magnificent, from the purely architectural point of view. Municipal pride, manifested by artistic embellishment without utilitarian purpose, shone out from them. They were built on generous grounds in what were then rural areas, outside the city bounds, on the theory that rustic peace had a healing effect upon fractured minds—and also that remoteness would protect the sane of the city from distressing contact with the insane. The city expanded and soon engulfed the asylums, but the grounds remained, often the only islands of green in a sea of soot and red brick. These grounds, right up until the asylums closed, were tended with a care that spoke of love and devotion.

For all who worked in them, the asylums provided a genuine sense of community. Indeed, by the time of their closure they were the only real communities for miles around, the surrounding society having been smashed into atoms. They held annual cricket matches and other sporting contests on their spacious lawns, and hosted summer and Christmas balls. The staff were often second- or third-generation employees, and the institution was central to their lives.

The patients benefited from the stability; the asylum was a little world in which they could behave as strangely as they pleased without anyone caring too much. They were free of the mockery and disdain with which people elsewhere would greet their strange demeanor, gestures, and ideas: for in the asylum, the strange was normal. Within its bounds, there was no stigma.

But of course there was a very dark side as well. Physical conditions, especially for those patients so chronically ill that the wards were in effect their homes, were appalling. There was no privacy, with beds sometimes packed so closely together that no one could walk between them. The smell of urine so deeply impregnated the furnishings and floors of the dayrooms that it seemed ineradicable (not that anyone tried to eradicate it). The stodgy food and physical inactivity meant that chronic constipation was universal; and most patients looked as if they had filtered their food through their shirts, blouses, and sweaters. Aimless wandering in the corridors was the principal recreation for many patients, who rarely saw a doctor, therapeutic impotence being more or less taken for granted. Individuals had lived in these conditions for more than half a century; and it was possible until the late 1980s to find women who had been committed to the asylums in the 1920s merely for having borne illegitimate children. As in the Soviet Union (though to a far less sinister degree), deviance was sometimes labeled madness and treated accordingly.

Most of the staff were kindly and well meaning, but, as in any situation in which some human beings have unsupervised care of and power over others, opportunities for sadism abounded. Usually these were minor: I often saw nurses denying cigarettes to patients, telling them to come back in a few minutes, for no other reason than the pleasure of exerting power over a fellow being. But from time to time far worse cruelty would surface, always hushed up in the name of institutional morale. This was easily done, since very few outside the asylum concerned themselves with what went on inside.

For most of their existence the asylums were custodial rather than therapeutic institutions. Their methods now strike us as laughably crude. One asylum doctor published a memoir just

after World War I in which he described how ʰ
leagues treated suicidal melancholics and agitat
They sat the melancholics against a wall, plac
front of them to prevent them from moving, wh
watched them to ensure that they did not do away with themselves. Croton oil, a very powerful laxative, subdued the agita-
tion of the paranoiacs, who became so preoccupied with the
movement of their bowels that they had no time or energy left
to act upon the content of their delusions.

Attempts at cures were often more desperate than well ad-
vised. One of the asylums of my city had the best-equipped op-
erating theater of its time, where an enthusiastic psychiatrist
partially eviscerated his patients and also removed all their
teeth, on the theory that madness was caused by a chronic but
undetected and subclinical infection (called "focal sepsis") in
the organs that he removed. Later a visiting neurosurgeon used
the theater to perform lobotomies on patients who were
scarcely aware of what was being done to them. Doctors also
tried more "advanced" treatments, such as insulin coma therapy, in which they gave schizophrenic patients insulin to lower
their blood sugar to the point at which they became unconscious, sometimes with fatal effect.

It was not difficult, then, to present asylums as chambers of
horrors, where bizarre sadistic rituals were carried out for reasons
unconnected with beneficent medical endeavor. And it so happened that one of the most powerful critics of both the asylum
system and psychiatry as a whole—powerful in the sense of having had the greatest overall effect—published his attack in 1961,
not long after the introduction of medications so efficacious in the
treatment of psychosis that the asylum populations had already
begun to decline, as patients were discharged back into the outside world. The name of the critic was Michel Foucault, and
within a few years his *Madness and Civilization* had spawned an
entire movement, though of somewhat disparate elements.

Foucault was not so much concerned by the cases of abuse or the poor conditions in asylums, as a mere reformer might have been. In the tortuous prose then typical of French intellectuals, he was concerned to assert that the separation of the mad from the sane, both physically and as a matter of classification, was neither intellectually justified nor motivated by beneficence. Instead it was an instance of the exertion of power by the rising bourgeoisie, which needed a disciplined and compliant workforce to fuel its economic system and was therefore increasingly intolerant of deviance—not only of conduct but of thought. It therefore locked deviants away in what Foucault called "the great incarceration" of the seventeenth and eighteenth centuries, of which the asylums of the Victorian Era were a late manifestation.

In Foucault's Nietzschean vision, all human institutions—even, or especially, those of avowedly beneficent intent—are expressions of the will to power, because such a will underlies all human activity. It is not really surprising, then, that asylums had turned into nothing but chambers of horrors: for psychiatry, and indeed the whole of medicine, to the rest of which Foucault soon turned his undermining attention, were not enterprises to liberate mankind from some of its travails—enterprises that inevitably committed errors en route to knowledge and enlightenment—but expressions of the will to power of the medical profession. The fact that this will was cloaked under an official ideology of benevolence made it only the more dangerous and sinister. This will needed to be unmasked so that mankind could liberate itself and live in the anarchic Dionysian mode that Foucault favored. (A sadomasochistic homosexual, the French philosopher later lived out his fantasies in San Francisco, and died of AIDS as a result.)

Foucault inspired subsequent critics of psychiatry, of varying degrees of scholarliness, rationality, and clarity of exposition. Among the best was the influential historian Andrew Scull, whose history of the origins of asylums, *Museums of Madness*, nevertheless implied that the arrogation of insanity to the purview of doctors in the eighteenth century did not grow out of any natural connection between the phenomena of madness and the endeavor of medicine—still less out of the practical ability of doctors of the time to cure madness (witness their failure in the case of George III)—but on the medical profession's entrepreneurial drive to increase its influence and income. The fact that the mad eventually came under the care of the medical profession was thus a historical accident, the result of the shrewd maneuvering of the doctors: some other group—the clergymen, for example, or the tailors—might have occupied the same position had they maneuvered as successfully. Founded on so illegitimate a basis, psychiatry was by implication a totally false undertaking.

This argument overlooks a few obvious facts, however. What could have been said of madness could have been said of dysentery and pneumonia—that the doctors of the time had no power to cure them and that therefore these diseases were not properly the province of physicians and might just as well have been handled by tinkers or topographers. If the Foucauldian style of thought had prevailed at earlier times, with that mindset's failure to understand imaginatively what is required to go from a state of complete ignorance to one of partial knowledge, and how it is often necessary to act in a state of ignorance, no one would ever have discovered anything about the cause or treatment of disease.

Moreover the connection between madness and medicine is not entirely arbitrary and unfounded, as Scull suggested (though in my opinion the scope of psychiatry has since expanded illegitimately, especially in the grotesque overprescription of psychotropic medication). The eighteenth-century doctors had in this respect a better grasp of reality than Professor Scull, for organic conditions leading to madness and dementia must have been very common at the time. It has been plausibly suggested (though not conclusively proved) that George III was suffering from porphyria, possibly exacerbated by lead poisoning, for instance, and at the end of the nineteenth century up to a quarter of the population of the asylums was suffering from general paralysis of the insane, the last stage of syphilis. Dare I mention that were it not for modern medicine, I myself would long ago have ended up in an asylum, one of those apathetic creatures that the physiognomists of madness in the nineteenth century so eloquently portrayed in their drawings, because I suffer from hypothyroidism, which is the most common of all endocrine diseases and which untreated can lead to madness and finally to dementia?

Another rhetorically powerful critic of psychiatry, also influenced by Foucault, was R. D. Laing, himself a psychiatrist. It was he who, in the 1960s and 1970s, gave currency to the idea that madness was an alternative, and in some ways superior, way of being in the world: that madness was in fact true sanity, and sanity true madness, insofar as the world itself was quite mad in its political, social, and domestic arrangements. According to Laing, it was the unequal power within families, and the distorted communications to which this inequality gave rise, that caused the condition in young people known as schizophrenia. To hospitalize them and treat them against their will was thus to punish them for the sins of their parents and to maintain an unjust social order at the same time.

This view became extremely popular in an era that uncritically criticized all institutions. The psychotic came to be viewed by right-thinking people as victims of injustice rather than as sufferers from illness (an attitude reinforced when it was discovered that young men of Jamaican origin living in Britain had a rate of schizophrenia six, seven, or eight times that of young white men). What was required was not treatment but restitution.

These ideas paved the way for an ill-conceived and hasty de-institutionalization of the mentally ill. Thanks to effective treatments, the numbers requiring to be institutionalized were declining anyway; politicians hoped to save money by deinstitutionalization and were all too willing to believe that the mentally ill could be managed almost without any institutions whatever; and finally, criticisms of the Foucauldian mold—that society had no right to impose restraint upon the mad—entered common consciousness. Madmen had a right to wander the streets, and other citizens had the duty to put up with it.

The asylums of my city closed within a few short years. The patients were sent to live in what bureaucrats insisted upon calling "the community," because of that term's connotations of warmth and welcome. With varying degrees of assistance and supervision, they were expected to live independently; they were given their autonomy, whether they wanted it or not. Many coped adequately with their newfound freedom, but many did not. And meanwhile, hospital provision for the mentally ill declined to such an extent, both for budgetary and ideological reasons (hospital admission was to be avoided at all costs, in a fetishistic kind of way, irrespective of the logic of the individual case), that every time it became imperatively necessary to admit a psychiatric patient, the entire system experienced a crisis. Madmen were left in police cells for days on end while hospital beds were found for them; sometimes, not a single such bed could be found in an area with a population of four or five million.

Every day in my work as a prison doctor I witnessed the effect of this lack of provision. Ironically the splendid new hospital wing of the prison, built with few expenses spared, rose on the grounds of an asylum that had just been closed down; but inside the hospital we were recreating the conditions of eighteenth-century Bedlam. Modern walls do not a modern hospital make. Unearthly screams rent the air; foul smells offended the nostrils.

Madmen threw their clothes through the windows, started fires in their cells, tore up their sheets, wrapped towels around their heads, angrily addressed their hallucinatory interlocutors while standing stark naked on their beds, refused all food as poisoned, and spat at passersby. All that was lacking were visitors from the outside world who had paid their pennies to laugh at the lunatics; I suggested that we reinstitute this great tradition to improve the prison's finances.

The cases would go like this: a madman would commit an offense—say, a completely unprovoked assault on a person in the street (unprovoked, that is, from the victim's point of view; the perpetrator would believe that the victim had been threatening or insulting him). The police would arrest him and take him to the police station. They would recognize that he was mad—his speech would be rambling and incoherent, he spoke of things that were not, and his behavior was completely beyond the bounds of reason. They would call a doctor, who would say that yes, the man was mad, but that no, he could not be admitted to a hospital to be treated, because there were no beds available.

The police then faced a dilemma. They could either release the man back into the community, whose sense of social solidarity he had so reinforced by his unprovoked attack on a random stranger, or they could charge him and put him before the courts. Sometimes they would do the one, sometimes the other. I have known lunatics released from police custody who clearly had intended to kill their victims in the street (and were handed back the weapons with which they intended to do it), because a policeman did not want to charge a man who was so obviously not responsible for his actions.

At other times, depending on who knows what factors, the police would bring the man before the courts, where a system of psychiatric screening had been set up. Theoretically the accused found to be psychiatrically unwell by the examining nurse would be diverted from the criminal justice system into the psychiatric system. But the nurse, knowing that no hospital beds would be available were she to declare the accused mentally ill, and not wishing to accept the labor of Hercules involved in trying to find such a bed, declares the madman (so mad that it requires no expertise at all to detect his madness) to be fully sane, or a malingerer, or to be currently under the influence of marijuana, so that his madness will pass within a short time and results from voluntary intoxication, which is no excuse under the law for his crime. Thus the madman is remanded into custody; and the nurse calms her conscience with the hope that the prison doctor will recognize the man's madness and will try to find a hospital bed for him.

Unfortunately, things do not go smoothly in the prison. The doctor cannot find a hospital bed for his mad patient; the psychiatrists outside the prison consider that the patient is now in a place of safety—the prison—where he will not be deprived of medical attention, and he is therefore of lower priority for a hospital bed than a lunatic still at large in the community. He is thus kept, often for months, in the prison on remand.

As the law now stands in Britain, prison doctors are not permitted to give treatment against a patient's will, except under the direst emergency, for fear they might abuse such power and forcibly sedate whomever they choose contrary to the patient's human rights. Hence psychotic patients are now kept in prison hospitals for months without any treatment whatsoever, thus taking part in an interesting if not altogether pleasing experiment in the natural history of psychosis, such as has not been conducted for many years.

Recently, for example, I observed a psychotic patient for several weeks, who addressed the world night and day through his prison window in words of muddled religious exaltation, who refused all food on the grounds that it was poisoned, his flesh melting away before my eyes, who attacked anyone who came within reach, and who painted religious slogans on the walls of his cell with his own excrement, thus imparting a nauseating feculent smell to the entire hospital.

It might, of course, be alleged that he behaved in so disturbed a fashion because he was incarcerated, and that his conduct was (in the opinion of R. D. Laing) a meaningful and enlightened response to his terrible social situation, and that he, of all the fourteen hundred prisoners in the prison, was acting in the most appropriate way under the circumstances. But this would be not only to ignore his medical history but also the fact that he was incarcerated in the first place because he had viciously and without provocation attacked a seventy-nine-year-old woman in a church, injuring her badly while reciting verses from the Bible, which suggests that his disturbed mental state preceded his incarceration and was not a consequence of it.

I checked the situation with lawyers. Although he had a fully documented history of psychosis and an entirely favorable response to treatment, attested to by both doctors and relatives (who said that when treated he was a pleasant and intelligent man), I was not entitled, in the name of human rights, to treat him against his will. In the name of human rights, therefore, the prison officers and the other prisoners had to endure weeks of revolting air, as well as disturbed nights in which sleep was all but impossible, while he lived in conditions that Hogarth might well have painted with justified moral fury.

The doctors to whom I proposed to send the patient accepted the conditions in which he lived with Buddha-like calm that would have been admirable had the suffering been theirs. Only the prison officers, among the most despised of all public servants, seemed to be moved by the scandal of the situation. The doctors, by contrast, were now so inured to such situations that they accepted it as normal and nothing to get excited about. The shortage of beds and the administrative difficulties that this shortage caused had steadily eroded their common humanity. It was only when I threatened to expose the scandal publicly and had taken photographs of the man's cell and said I would send them to the government minister responsible for prisons (a proceeding completely against the rules, but supported by the prison warden, who did not want his prison turned into a surrogate lunatic asylum) that the man was finally found a place in a hospital, where he could be treated.

Of course Foucault might have put a completely different construction on the outrage of the prison officers and the desire of the man's relatives for him to be treated and returned to normality. He might have interpreted all this as an intolerant refusal to accept the man's alternative way of life, a refusal even to try to interpret the meaning of the communications that he coded in his own excrement. For Foucault, their concern, couched in the terms of humanity, concealed a drive for power and domination, used to produce conformity to debilitating and dehumanizing bourgeois standards. But such an interpretation would surely mean that common humanity and a feeling for others are qualities whose very possibility he would radically deny: that the only relations that could exist between men are those of power, and that all else is illusion.

I am aware that hard cases make bad law, but I could cite many such cases like the one above; of cases, for example, where doctors have changed their diagnoses in order to avoid the responsibility of finding hospital beds for their patients, and where they have even perjured themselves in court to evade that responsibility, to the great detriment of the patient and the safety of society alike. These are now part of everyday practice.

The shortage of beds, brought about by the desire to make financial savings in the context of an ideological assault on the notion of psychiatric illness, has corrupted doctors and nurses by slow but inexorable steps.

I am also aware that many horror stories could be told of doctors who have been overzealous (to put it mildly) in their attempts to cure their patients or to spread their fields of operations to their own material and social advantage. There is no simple formula for avoiding the Scylla of zealotry on the one hand and the Charybdis of abandonment of responsibility on the other. The art is long, life is short, the occasion fleeting, and judgment difficult. But the difficulty must be faced.

One thing is certain: that Foucault and his ilk are no guides to how to treat a man like the one I have described (and such as I have come across every day). Should he have been let free to continue his Dionysian assaults on defenseless old ladies, on the grounds that they were life-enhancing? I cannot see that this represents anything but a preference for barbarism.

2005

A Murderess's Tale

◆ IT IS A FICTION—a socially necessary one, perhaps, but a fiction nonetheless—that all murderers are created equal. They are not. Though murder is the worst crime, murderers are not necessarily the worst criminals. In fact, contact with many of them has taught me that it is possible to abominate the crime without always abominating the criminal.

Man being a fallen creature, momentary and uncharacteristic lapses do occur. Moreover the law's doctrine that provocation or duress can count as an exculpating excuse only if it has immediately preceded the crime is psychologically unrealistic, though it is perhaps another socially necessary fiction. Many a straw, after all, has broken many a camel's back; and sometimes I have found myself thinking, when listening to a murderer, that I am not sure that I would have acted so very differently had I been in his place.

Moreover, murderers are, of all criminals, the most prone to genuine remorse and self-reproach. Burglars rarely reproach themselves; rather, they are full of condemnation of others, from parents and police to physicians and politicians. But even murderers whose whole lives have, in retrospect, been but a preamble to murder experience a change of heart once they have killed. Their murder acts on them like a religious conversion (to which, indeed, it is sometimes a prelude); and while some killers remain psychopathically indifferent to their crimes, they are relatively few. I have met Hannibal Lecter types, but not often.

Every murder raises deep and disturbing questions, philosophical, psychological, and sociological: none more so than one in which I recently gave testimony in court. The accused was a girl aged eighteen, who had stabbed her sixteen-year-old lesbian lover to death. There could be no doubt as to who had inflicted the fatal wounds: a tape from a closed-circuit camera in the entrance hall of the accused's apartment building showed her following her lover out of the building with a long knife in each hand, raised ready to stab, as in a too-melodramatic rendition of Lady Macbeth.

Under English law, then, only two defenses were left to her: insanity or diminished responsibility. There was no question of insanity, however. She was not, nor did she claim to be, mad. Her lawyer argued for diminished responsibility, a plea that would have made her guilty of the lesser crime of manslaughter, rather than murder. While murder carries a mandatory life sentence, manslaughter allows the judge considerable discretion as to sentence: anything from an unconditional release to life in prison. The verdict is therefore worth arguing for.

But what is diminished responsibility? The Homicide Act of 1957 introduced it as a defense to the charge of murder, as a compromise with those who wished to abolish the death penalty altogether (as was enacted nine years later). The act states that a person is guilty of manslaughter, not murder, if he suffered at the time from a state of mind that substantially impaired his mental responsibility for his actions. As to what constitutes such a state of mind, a judge ruled that it was a state so different from a normal state of mind that an ordinary person—that is to say, a member of a jury—would accept it as such. But while it is for a jury to decide the question, in practice medical evidence plays a decisive role. In this case I appeared for the prosecution: though, as I shall explain, with a heavy heart.

On the day in question, the perpetrator and her victim, who had spent the night together, rose at about one in the afternoon. This was perfectly normal for them: they were both unemployed, and they had spent the evening before (as they always did) drinking to excess and smoking marijuana. Once they had risen, the victim went to the nearest store to buy more alcohol, in the form of cheap, strong cider, sold in two- or three-liter bottles to alcoholics—no one else drinks it.

They spent the afternoon drinking and smoking more marijuana together. Then, as so often happens when people combine drugs and alcohol, an argument broke out between them. Participants describe such arguments as existing independently of those who have them—more like a meteorological phenomenon than a human one. As the accused put it, the argument got out of hand, though she could not remember exactly, or even approximately, what it was about. She went to the kitchen to fetch a knife (actually, two knives) and then returned to her lover. Her intention, as she remembered it, was to encourage her to leave the apartment, which she did. Unfortunately, very shortly afterward, the accused followed her, and the rest was homicide. The killer called for an ambulance, and her teenage lover all but bled to death in her arms. Her last words were "It hurts" and "I'm tired."

Relations between the victim and perpetrator, which had begun three years earlier, since they were thirteen and fifteen, respectively, had always been difficult, with many drug- and alcohol-fueled quarrels, often ending up with the waving of knives and other weapons. The victim's mother said that she had always thought it would end in murder.

The issue in court was whether the killer had what is known in our overmedicalized world as a personality disorder, or what used to be called a bad character. The World Health Organization defines personality disorders as "extreme or significant deviations from the way the average individual in a given culture perceives, thinks, feels and, particularly, relates to others. Such behavior patterns tend to be stable and to encompass multiple domains of behavior and psychological functioning. They are frequently, but not always, associated with various degrees of subjective distress and problems of social performance." The diagnosis thus rests upon vague criteria, of doubtful validity; but it makes sense, more or less, in practice.

If the accused had such a disorder, and her actions could plausibly be attributed to it, the defense might argue that she therefore did indeed have diminished responsibility for her actions: for it is accepted without argument today that a man is not in the least responsible for his own personality or character—a far cry from Marcus Aurelius's view two thousand years ago that a man could, and ought to, cultivate his own character.

The use of personality disorder in such cases seems to me to be little else than a thin or even frivolous pretext for leniency, for if the argument were taken seriously it would lead to *more* severe punishment rather than less. If a man kills as a result of a momentary but understandable lapse, in unusual circumstances, he is guilty of murder but is unlikely to kill again; if a man kills because his character is deficient, and it is therefore the kind of thing he does, he is guilty of manslaughter but, *ex hypothesi*, is likely to do it again.

Not long ago I testified in a case in which personality disorder served as an illogical pretext for leniency. A woman in her early forties, an alcoholic, had married another alcoholic and had a child by him. The father subsequently gave up drinking, separated from his wife—who continued to drink—and came to the conclusion that she was not a suitable mother for his child. He was in the process of applying for custody.

By now the child was two years old. One day the mother—probably drunk—dissolved the contents of her anti-depressant capsules in some cough medicine and injected the solution into the child's mouth with a syringe. The child died as a result.

Against my arguments, the jury accepted that her supposed personality disorder had diminished her responsibility, and the judge sentenced her to three years' probation (she had already spent a year in prison by the time the case came to court). Oddly enough, in arguing that she was guilty of the more serious crime of murder rather than the less serious one of manslaughter, I was also arguing that she was less dangerous in the future than her own defense implied. I strongly suspect that, while drunk, she had said to herself something like, "If I can't have my child, no one else will," and had resorted to the pills with the very kind of premeditation that makes someone guilty of murder (the dissolution of her capsules and her administration of them to her daughter could hardly have been the result of a momentary lapse, after all). But since she was unlikely ever to have another child, she posed little further danger to society: the circumstances in which she killed would never arise again. There was a paradox, therefore: for the greater crime meant the lesser danger, and the lesser crime the greater danger. But the greater crime carried a penalty of mandatory severity, which seemed disproportionate to the jury, and they could avoid it only by resort to intellectual dishonesty.

In my opinion there was no question of personality disorder in the case of the young murderess. When I visited her in prison to prepare my report to the court, I discovered—to my own great surprise, I must confess—that far from being a person of bad character, she was of good character. Or perhaps I should say: would have been of good character had someone offered her a little loving guidance earlier in her life. For if anyone could ever have blamed her upbringing for her crime, she could have. What was impressive about her—moving even—was her steadfast refusal to do so. She blamed herself, and herself alone.

Of mixed race, she was the youngest of three children by a man who deserted her mother immediately after her birth. Apparently he had been a violent wastrel, and, as is so often the case, the mother took up soon afterward with another man of the same type but even worse—a crack-smoking criminal who was in and out of prison. When at liberty, he neither worked nor provided for any of the children (her mother had a further two children by him, making five so far).

Jealous and possessive, he was extremely violent to her mother, accusing her of having had affairs with other men while he was in prison. He broke her jaw, her ribs, and her arm on separate occasions. Sometimes she would flee from him, taking the children with her to shelters, but either he would find her and intimidate her into returning, or she would grow nostalgic for his embraces and come back to him herself. It was hardly surprising in the circumstances that the killer-to-be's education was patchy. Thanks to her mother's attempts to evade her lover, followed by reconciliations both voluntary and involuntary, the girl attended almost as many schools as she had years of formal education.

One of the characteristics of relationships such as that between her mother and her stepfather is their all-consuming nature, at least for the woman. She can think of, and has time for, nothing else: she is the star, albeit the unhappy one, of her own mental soap opera. In this case the mother noticed neither the stepfather's habitual violence toward her children by her former lover nor the fact that her oldest son was having intercourse with her daughter while the boy was between the ages of thirteen and seventeen, and his sister was between the ages of eight and twelve.

Eventually her daughter, now fourteen, plucked up the courage to tell her what had happened. Her mother said she didn't believe her, flew into a rage, and threw her out of the house. She went to stay with a friend and then asked her mother whether she could return home. As a condition of doing so, her mother made her apologize to her brother and swear never to say anything like it again.

Her mother also failed to notice that, from the age of twelve, her daughter had begun to drink heavily: or if she noticed it, she considered it a matter of no importance. Her daughter skipped school in order to drink; by the evening, she was often very drunk and soon got to the stage when she drank first thing in the morning to steady her shaking hands. She was also smoking marijuana. She said that she drank and smoked to obliterate the reality of her life, which was too awful to bear unaided.

When she was fifteen, she went herself to the Social Services Department and asked to be taken away from her home, to escape its atmosphere of violence and intimidation. The department put her into a children's home, where an atmosphere of violence also prevailed: drug taking and sexual predation set the tone.

It was here that she formed a lesbian relationship with a thirteen-year-old who lived nearby. Neither the Social Services officials who ran the home nor the parents of the thirteen-year-old (who came from a background similar to her eventual killer's) were sufficiently in control to prevent the relationship from developing.

While the girl was in the children's home, her mother finally broke with the violent, criminal, crack-smoking stepfather and at once took up with a man fifteen years her junior. She immediately "caught pregnant," as they say around here, and had her sixth child, whereupon her young lover did the usual thing in the circumstances and abandoned her to the care of the taxpayers. In the welfare state, experience teaches nothing.

Social Services regarded the killer-to-be, at the age of sixteen, as ready to stand on her own two feet, at least with regard to daily living, and gave her a furnished apartment of her own. She neither went to college—impossible because of her poor education—nor worked, since the various subventions she received, such as free rent and exemption from local taxes, made that not only unnecessary but uneconomic. So she spent her days in drunken and marijuana-intoxicated idleness, living intermittently with her underage lover. The two of them became the heroines of their own mental soap opera. Their quarrels and reconciliations became the focus of their whole existence, the very violence of their scenes being evidence (as far as they were concerned) of their importance and significance. And then one scene ended in murder.

When I went to see her in prison, the young killer was prey to the most profound remorse. It was several months after she had killed. She was obviously of good intelligence, though as badly educated as most in her station in life, despite the state's unprecedentedly large expenditures on free and compulsory education. She wept bitterly when speaking of her crime, but not self-pityingly. She had carved the name of her dead lover on her flesh, but in no exhibitionist or histrionic spirit. She said she wanted henceforth to be good, to behave well, for the sake of the deceased. She wanted to make something of herself, that she might travel, which had always been the ambition of her dead lover. She would never drink or smoke marijuana again.

She said that prison had done her much good; it was the first place in which she had ever felt truly settled. She was going to classes to improve her English and math. She had been treated well and fairly, and felt much better both physically and mentally. I checked with the staff: she was noted for her politeness and pleasant manner. This was just as I had found her.

Although she was distressed when, at my prompting, she recounted her life to me, she never attempted in the slightest degree to insinuate that her experiences were responsible for or explained her crime (although she was still only eighteen, they were surely far more than any person should ever have to experience). She said, "It's terrible that it had to come to this for me to take my own life seriously." She meant it, if anyone ever meant anything; and hers were not the words of someone with a serious personality disorder but, on the contrary, of someone with a surprisingly robust and decent character.

Toward the end of our very long interview, I asked her whether there was anything she wanted to ask me. She said that there was.

"What is it?" I inquired.

"Have you ever been to a trial before?" she said.

"Yes, many times."

"Can you tell me, will they be nasty to me?"

At this point I felt a deep pang of sorrow: for her question was a child's question. For all the precocity forced upon her, for all the street credibility she had no doubt assumed for the sake of survival in the brutal urban environment in which she found herself, for all the pseudo-independence thrust upon her by her feckless mother and Social Services, she was still a child, not an adult.

As I left the prison, convinced that from the purely legal standpoint she had been guilty of murder and not of manslaughter, I pondered the question of why she had found prison so good, one might almost say so liberating, an experience. (She was far from unique in this regard, incidentally.)

The answer must be that for the first time in her life she was set limits: limits that, while imposed, were intrinsically reasonable and were not therefore arbitrary or dependent upon whim. Both keeping to those limits and breaking them produced entirely predictable consequences, good or bad. For the first time in her life she had entered a world in which things made sense, in which brute power did not determine everything. As she might have put it herself, it was a pity that she had to go to prison to be treated with consistent decency.

The prison was a long way from my home, and as I drove I thought about the meaning of this terrible story. What would a liberal say about it? How would he explain what had happened? How would he go about trying to ensure that such cases did not recur?

Would he say that the state had been insufficiently generous with its Social Security payments, as a result of which the murderess had suffered material deprivations that caused her to commit her crime? But her mother had brought six children into the world, all by men who had contributed not a single penny to their upkeep. The murderess had never gone without food, was of notably strong physique, was of good stature, had never been ill, and had probably never even gone a day of her life without hot water. She was well clothed, and though she had never worked a single day of her life, her home boasted a stove, a refrigerator, a VCR, a stereo, and no doubt many other appurtenances that would have made Nero gasp. What more should the state have done or given her in the way of material goods?

Was she the victim of a restrictive sexual code that frustrated her desires and caused her to become violent? Surely even the most liberal of liberals would blush to say so. As she was incestuously raped from the age of eight to twelve, and was herself able to take up a lesbian relationship with a girl aged thirteen completely unopposed either by the state or by private individuals, it is difficult to see how further sexual license could have saved the day.

Had the educational system stifled her self-esteem? Quite the reverse. Our schools have fulfilled the liberal educators' every dream, abandoning educational achievement as their goal and systematically replacing it with nurturing self-esteem—or at least self-conceit—leaving their pupils unaware of their own disastrous ignorance, unable even to read properly, and without a counterweight to their chaotic home environments. Perhaps if the accused, and all the young people around her, had been treated with a firm but benevolent guiding hand when they were younger, the tragedy might have been averted.

Was the criminal justice system too harsh, above all on her stepfather? On her own account, he was never accused or found guilty of more than a very small fraction of the crimes that he had actually committed. Moreover he was repeatedly released from prison, though he had provided irrefutable evidence that he had absolutely no intention of changing his mode of life. Had he been kept in prison for as long as he so manifestly deserved, there would have been at least the possibility that his "family" might have achieved a modicum of stability.

Was the problem that the killer was unable to obtain alcohol and marijuana easily enough? Had they been available to her freely, and free of charge, from (say) the age of six, would the tragedy have been averted?

Or perhaps she was released from the children's home at too tender an age? But the demand that adolescents be treated as autonomous adults has never been a conservative one, because it seems to conservatives to be not in accordance with human experience; rather, it is a liberal demand.

This murder, exceptional in some characteristics as it undoubtedly was, took place in a social universe that liberals have wrought, and whose realities they are too guilty or cowardly to acknowledge. It is a universe that has no place for children or childhood in it. Believing that man is the product of his environment, they have nevertheless set about creating an environment from which it is truly difficult to escape, by closing off all the avenues and bolt-holes as far as possible. They have destroyed the family and any notion of progress or improvement. They have made a world in which the only freedom is self-indulgence, a world from which—most terrible of all—prison can sometimes be a liberation.

2005

Index